VEGETABLE BASICS

MY COOKING CLASS

VEGETABLE BASICS

84 RECIPES ILLUSTRATED STEP BY STEP

JODY VASSALLO

PHOTOGRAPHS BY CLIVE BOZZARD-HILL

✳ ✳ ✳

FIREFLY BOOKS

A FIREFLY BOOK

Published by Firefly Books Ltd. 2010

First printing

Publisher Cataloging-in-Publication Data (U.S.)
Vassallo, Jody.
    Vegetable basics : 84 recipes illustrated step by step / Jody Vassallo ; photographs by Clive Bozzard-Hill.
[256] p. : col. photos. ; cm.
Includes index.
ISBN-13: 978-1-55407-760-1 (pbk.)
ISBN-10: 1-55407-760-5 (pbk.)
    1. Cookery (Vegetables). I. Bozzard-Hill, Clive. II. Title.
641.65 dc22   TX801.V3773 2010

Library and Archives Canada Cataloguing in Publication
Vassallo, Jody
    Vegetable basics : 84 recipes illustrated step by step / Jody Vassallo.
Includes index.
ISBN-13: 978-1-55407-760-1 (pbk.)
ISBN-10: 1-55407-760-5 (pbk.)
    1. Cookery (Vegetables). I. Title.
TX801.V375 2010   641.6'5   C2010-901578-9

Published in the United States by
Firefly Books (U.S.) Inc.
P.O. Box 1338, Ellicott Station
Buffalo, New York 14205

Published in Canada by
Firefly Books Ltd.
66 Leek Crescent
Richmond Hill, Ontario L4B 1H1

Printed in China

INTRODUCTION

You probably grew up as I did, with a mother assuring you that you wouldn't grow up to be big and strong if you didn't eat all your vegetables. My evening meal always consisted of vegetables, and as many of them as Mom could possibly persuade me to eat. Well, I now congratulate her on her supreme effort. I am a woman who loves my vegetables. In fact, I'd have to say about 80 percent of my meals consist of only vegetables; I find them so versatile and completely satisfying. I found so much joy in writing and testing all the recipes in this book, and I got to know some vegetables I had never met before, like salsify and samphire. I experimented with different cooking methods, and I also rediscovered some mouthwatering traditional favorites.

I was reminded that vegetables have been a cornerstone of society for hundreds of years, and I learned many new ways to persuade my not-so-vegetable-loving friends to include them in their daily diet. Who could say no to a plate of scrambled eggs befriending creamed spinach? Show me anyone who can resist a hearty bowl of minestrone in winter, or a plate of broad beans fighting for center stage with sliced chorizo. And I dare anyone to find a friend who won't scrape their plate of mushroom risotto clean.

✳ ✳ ✳

CONTENTS

1
ROOTS & TUBERS

2
FRUIT-LIKE VEGETABLES

3
CABBAGE

4
STALKS, SHOOTS & THISTLES

5
MUSHROOMS

6
ONIONS

7
LEAFY VEGETABLES

8
PODS & SEEDS

9
DESSERTS & BEVERAGES

APPENDIXES

ROOTS & TUBERS

1

Classic Potato Croquettes 1
French Fries 2
Potatoes Dauphinoise 3
Potato Rösti 4
Roast Potatoes 5
Patatas Bravas 6
Potato Gnocchi 7
Carrot Hummus 8
Jerusalem Artichoke Soup 9
Roast Parsnips & Carrots 10
Oven-Roasted Vegetables 11
Sweet Potato Chips 12
Sweet Potato Crumble 13
Beet & Cheese Salad 14
Seven-Vegetable Tagine 15
Potato Smash 16
Parsnip Mash 16
Celeriac Puree 17
Sweet Potato Mash 17
Indian Vegetable Curry 18

CLASSIC POTATO CROQUETTES

SERVES: 4 • PREPARATION: 20 MINUTES, PLUS 1 HOUR TO CHILL • COOKING: 20 MINUTES

2¼ pounds (1 kg) floury potatoes, peeled and chopped into even-sized pieces
2 garlic cloves, peeled
⅔ cup (150 ml) unsalted butter, chopped
1 cup (250 ml) milk

Sea salt and black pepper, to taste
10 ounces (300 g) Gruyère or Emmentaler cheese, finely grated
2 tablespoons (30 ml) chopped herbs, such as thyme, parsley and oregano

1 cup (250 ml) all-purpose flour
3 eggs, lightly beaten
½ cup (125 ml) dried breadcrumbs
Vegetable oil, for deep-frying

1 2
3 4

1	Boil the potatoes and garlic until soft. Drain well and return to the pot. Heat through to remove excess water.	2	Add the butter, milk (see notes on following page), salt and pepper to the potatoes, return to the heat and cook until the butter is melted.
3	Mash until smooth and creamy. You can stop here if you just want mashed potatoes.	4	Add the cheese and beat with hand-held electric beaters until the potatoes are soft and creamy. ➢

5	Transfer the mashed potatoes to a bowl, add the herbs and any flavorings (see notes, opposite) and stir to combine.	6	Shape the croquettes using 2 tablespoons (30 ml) of the mixture at a time. Chill in the refrigerator for 30 minutes to 1 hour, or until firm.
7	Put the flour, eggs and bread crumbs in 3 bowls and coat the croquettes first in the flour, then in the eggs and lastly in the bread crumbs.	8	Heat the oil for deep-frying in a deep saucepan and deep-fry the croquettes until crisp and golden. Drain on paper towels.

9	Serve the croquettes with a salad.	**NOTES** ❁ Use only ½ to ¾ cup (125 to 175ml) milk if you are going to make croquettes, as you want the mixture to be a little firmer than if you are making mashed potato. You can also add smoked salmon, ham or salami with the herbs in step 5.

FRENCH FRIES

❧ SERVES: 4 • PREPARATION: 30 MINUTES • COOKING: 30 MINUTES ❧

2¼ pounds (1 kg) potatoes, peeled
Vegetable oil, for deep-frying

Sea salt to taste
Mayonnaise or ketchup, to serve

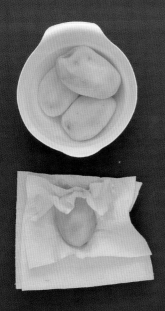

1 2
3 4

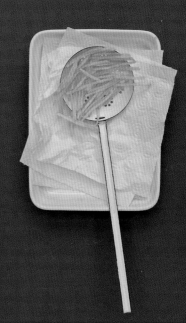

1	Soak the potatoes in cold water to remove the starch. Pat dry with paper towels.	2	Cut the potatoes into 2-inch (5 cm) thick pieces.	
3	Heat the oil in a deep saucepan and deep-fry the potatoes in batches for 1 minute.	4	Remove and drain on paper towels.	➤

5	Return the fries to the saucepan in batches and deep-fry until crisp and golden. Drain on paper towels.	**NOTE** ❋ You can pre-cook the fries, deep-frying them the first time 2 hours ahead of time then frying a second time just before serving. For best results cook the fries in batches.

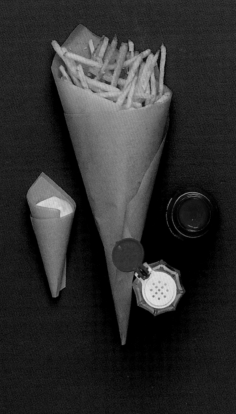

			VARIATION
	Sprinkle with salt and serve with mayonnaise or ketchup.		❊
6			You can cut the potatoes into thicker strips or wedges and follow the same method; they will take a little longer to cook than regular French fries.

POTATOES DAUPHINOISE

❖ SERVES: 4 TO 6 • PREPARATION: 15 MINUTES • COOKING: 50 TO 60 MINUTES ❖

2¼ pounds (1 kg) potatoes, peeled
1 large or 2 small onions
2½ cups (625 ml) heavy (36%) cream

Sea salt and black pepper, to taste
2 chicken bouillon cubes

1 2
3 4

1	Preheat the oven to 400°F (200°C). Cut the potatoes and onions into thin slices.	2	Layer the potato and onion slices into a 1½-quart (1.5 L) baking dish.
3	Season the cream with salt, pepper and the bouillon cubes and pour over the potatoes and onions.	4	Bake for 50 to 60 minutes, or until the potatoes are soft and the top is golden.

POTATO RÖSTI

❧ SERVES: 4 (MAKES: 12) • PREPARATION: 20 MINUTES • COOKING: 30 MINUTES ❧

1½ pounds (750 g) floury potatoes, peeled
1 medium onion
½ cup (125 ml) sunflower oil

3 tablespoons (45 ml) butter
Sea salt, to taste

TO SERVE:
Smoked salmon
Watercress
Sour cream

1 2
3 4

1	Grate the potatoes and onion separately.	2	Put the potatoes into a clean tea towel and squeeze out any excess moisture.	
3	Put the potatoes and onion in a bowl and mix together. Shape into flat patties using 2 table-spoons (30 ml) of the mixture at a time.	4	Heat the oil and butter in a frying pan and brown the rösti over medium heat, flipping to crisp both sides.	➢

5	Drain the cooked rösti on paper towels. Season with salt.	**VARIATION** ❈ Try adding finely chopped fresh herbs or finely shredded ham to the rösti mixture. You can also serve the rösti with bacon and eggs for breakfast or with chargrilled meats at lunch or dinner.

6

Serve with smoked salmon, watercress and sour cream.

NOTE
※

You can make a large, pan-sized rösti, but you will need extra butter and oil to cook it. To turn the rösti over, slide it onto a plate then put it back into the pan raw-side down and continue to fry until golden brown.

ROAST POTATOES

➤ SERVES: 4 • PREPARATION: 20 MINUTES • COOKING: 40 MINUTES ➤

1½ pounds (750 g) floury potatoes, peeled
  and cut into large chunks
Sea salt
Olive oil

1 2
3 4

1	Preheat oven to 400°F (200°C). Boil the potatoes in boiling water until just soft. Drain, then return them to the pot and heat to remove excess water.	2	Remove the potatoes from the pot and use a fork to score the surface of the potatoes.
3	Put the potatoes in a roasting pan, sprinkle with salt and drizzle with oil.	4	Bake until crisp and golden. Serve with roasted or chargrilled meats.

PATATAS BRAVAS

✦ SERVES: 4 TO 6 • PREPARATION: 10 MINUTES • COOKING: 40 MINUTES ✦

2¼ pounds (1 kg) potatoes
Vegetable oil, for shallow-frying
2 tablespoons (30 ml) olive oil

1 red onion, finely chopped
3 garlic cloves, finely chopped
2 small dried red chilies, finely chopped
  (see note)

1 teaspoon (5 ml) paprika
1 pound (500 g) ripe tomatoes, finely
  chopped (about 1½ cups/375 ml)

1 2
3 4

1	Boil the potatoes until soft, allow to cool slightly then peel. Cut into large pieces.	2	Heat the vegetable oil in a frying pan, and fry the potatoes in batches until crisp and golden. Drain on paper towels.	
3	Heat the olive oil in another frying pan and fry the onion, garlic and chilies for 5 minutes, or until the onion is soft.	4	Add the paprika and chopped tomatoes to the pan. Bring to a boil and cook until the sauce is reduced by half.	➤

5	Transfer the sauce to a food processor or blender and process until smooth.	**VARIATION** ✳ For a richer sauce, stir ⅓ cup (75 ml) of mayonnaise through the tomato sauce, or you can serve the mayonnaise on top of the potatoes with the spicy tomato sauce.

	Serve the fried potatoes topped with the tomato sauce.	**NOTE** ✽
6		Use only 1 dried chili if you want a less spicy sauce. Leftover sauce can be kept in the refrigerator for up to 3 days.

POTATO GNOCCHI

❖ SERVES: 4 • PREPARATION: 1 HOUR • COOKING: 40 MINUTES ❖

2¼ pounds (1 kg) floury potatoes,
  scrubbed
1 egg

2 cups (500 ml) Italian type 00 flour or
  organic all-purpose flour
Sea salt and pepper, to taste

TO SERVE:
Tomato sauce (see recipe 19)
Grated pecorino cheese, to taste
Basil leaves, to garnish

1 2
3 4

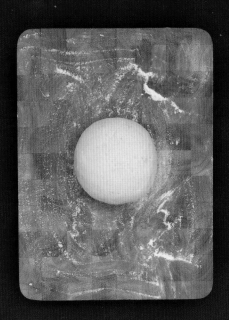

1	Boil the potatoes until soft. Drain and peel off the skins.	2	Roughly chop the potatoes then mash them in a food mill. If you don't have a food mill, mash them with a potato masher.	
3	Add the egg and mix to combine. Add 1 cup (250 ml) of flour and season with salt and pepper. Mix until smooth.	4	Sprinkle the remaining flour onto a board, then knead the dough to form a smooth ball.	➤

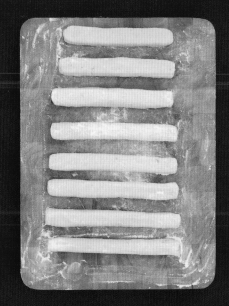

5 6
7 8

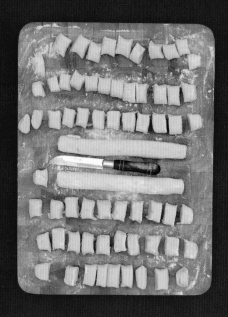

5	Cut the dough ball into 8 pieces.	6	Roll each portion into a long, thin sausage shape.
7	Cut off small sections of the dough with a sharp knife.	8	Boil the gnocchi in lightly salted water for 2 minutes, or until they float to the surface. Remove them with a slotted spoon.

9 | Serve the gnocchi with your favorite sauce. For example, a tomato pasta sauce (see recipe 19) finished with grated pecorino cheese and a few basil leaves.

TIP
❋

Cooked gnocchi can be frozen and then boiled from frozen, if desired; it will take about 5 minutes to cook.

CARROT HUMMUS

⇒ SERVES: 6 • PREPARATION: 15 MINUTES • COOKING: 30 MINUTES ⇐

1 pound (500 g) carrots, peeled
1 (14–ounce/398 ml) can chickpeas
2 garlic cloves, peeled

2 tablespoons (30 ml) tahini
1 teaspoon (5 ml) ground cumin
3 tablespoons (45 ml) lemon juice

2 tablespoons (30 ml) olive oil
1 tablespoon (15 ml) Greek yogurt
Pita bread, to serve

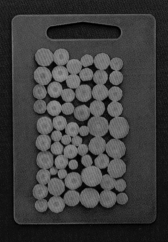

1 2
3 4

1	Boil the carrots until tender. Drain well and roughly chop.	2	Put the carrots, chickpeas, garlic, tahini, cumin, lemon juice, olive oil and yogurt in a food processor.
3	Process until smooth.	4	Serve the carrot hummus with pita bread.

JERUSALEM ARTICHOKE SOUP

❖ SERVES: 4 • PREPARATION: 20 MINUTES • COOKING: 40 MINUTES ❖

1 pound (500 g) Jerusalem artichokes
1 tablespoon (15 ml) lemon juice
3 garlic cloves, peeled
⅓ cup (75 ml) heavy (36%) cream

Sea salt and black pepper, to taste
1 tablespoon (15 ml) olive oil
1 teaspoon (5 ml) fennel seeds
1 chorizo, sliced

½ teaspoon (2 ml) smoked paprika
2 cups (500 ml) chicken stock
Sour cream, to serve

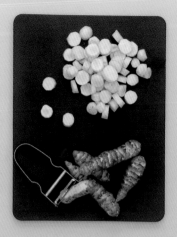

1 2
3 4

1	Peel and chop the Jerusalem artichokes. Put them in water with the lemon juice to prevent discoloring.	2	Boil the artichokes and garlic until soft, then drain. Return to heat, add the cream and cook until it is about to boil. Puree in a blender or food processor and season.
3	Heat the oil in a frying pan, add the fennel and chorizo and cook until browned. Stir in the paprika. Return the puree to the pan, add the stock and boil.	4	Serve the soup topped with the fennel and chorizo and a little sour cream.

ROAST PARSNIPS & CARROTS

⤖ SERVES: 4 • PREPARATION: 10 MINUTES • COOKING: 40 MINUTES ⬳

1 pound (500 g) small parsnips
½ pound (250 g) baby carrots
½ pound (250 g) French shallots
2 tablespoons (30 ml) olive oil

Cracked black and pink peppercorns, to
  taste
3 sprigs rosemary
3 tablespoons (45 ml) maple syrup

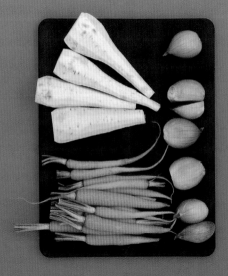

1 2
3 4

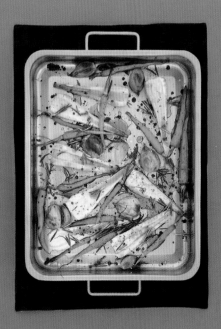

1	Preheat oven to 400°F (200°C). Scrub the parsnips and carrots using a small vegetable brush. Peel the shallots.	2	Cut the parsnips in half and put them in a large roasting pan together with the carrots and shallots.
3	Drizzle oil over, then sprinkle peppercorns and rosemary over. Bake for 40 minutes, or until soft and golden.	4	Drizzle maple syrup over and serve with roasted meats.

OVEN-ROASTED VEGETABLES

❖ SERVES: 4 • PREPARATION: 20 MINUTES • COOKING: 50 MINUTES ❖

2 lemons, cut into wedges
2 leeks, cut into 2-inch (5cm) pieces
2 red peppers, chopped
1 pound (500 g) carrots, cut into wedges
1 head garlic, halved

10 ounces (300 g) sweet potato, peeled and cut into large pieces
1 large rutabaga, peeled and cut into large pieces
8 ounces (250 g) baby potatoes

14 ounces (400 g) cherry tomatoes on the vine
⅓ cup (75 ml) olive oil
Sea salt and black pepper, to taste
Thyme and oregano sprigs, to garnish

1 2
3 4

1	Preheat oven to 400°F (200°C). Put the lemons and vegetables, except the tomatoes, in a roasting pan, drizzle half the oil over and bake for 40 minutes.	2	Add the tomatoes and bake for a further 10 minutes, or until the tomatoes' skins burst.
3	Peel the garlic and scatter over the roasted vegetables.	4	Season with salt and pepper. Drizzle the remaining oil, the juice squeezed from the baked lemons and garnish with herbs. Serve.

SWEET POTATO CHIPS

❧ SERVES: 4 • PREPARATION: 15 MINUTES • COOKING: 15 MINUTES ❧

1½ pounds (750 g) sweet potatoes
1 teaspoon (5 ml) sea salt
2 tablespoons (30 ml) toasted sesame seeds

1 teaspoon (5 ml) finely grated lime zest
Vegetable oil, for deep-frying

1 2
3 4

1	Use a sharp vegetable peeler to peel the sweet potatoes and slice them into long strips.	2	Put the sea salt, sesame seeds and lime juice into a mortar and gently crush with a pestle to split the sesame seeds.
3	Heat the oil in a saucepan and cook the sweet potatoes in batches until golden. Drain and keep the chips warm while you continue cooking.	4	Spinkle the sesame seed mixture over the sweet potato chips and serve.

SWEET POTATO CRUMBLE

➤ SERVES: 4 • PREPARATION: 30 MINUTES • COOKING: 30 MINUTES ➤

1½ pounds (750 g) sweet potatoes, peeled
2 garlic cloves, peeled
1 tablespoon (15 ml) grated ginger
1 cup (250 ml) coarse bread crumbs

½ cup (125 ml) pecans, roughly chopped
3 tablespoons (45 ml) butter, chopped
½ teaspoon (2 ml) ground cinnamon
2 teaspoons (10 ml) honey

1 tablespoon (15 ml) chopped mixed herbs,
  such as oregano, sage, thyme
2 tablespoons (30 ml) olive oil
Sea salt and black pepper, to taste

1 2
3 4

1	Preheat oven to 400°F (200°C). Boil the sweet potatoes, garlic and ginger until soft. Drain well and mash.	2	Mix together the bread crumbs, pecans, butter, cinnamon, honey, herbs and oil and season with salt and pepper.
3	Spoon the mashed sweet potatoes into a greased 1½-quart (1.5 L) baking dish and sprinkle the crumb mixture over them.	4	Bake for 30 minutes, or until crisp and golden.

BEET & CHEESE SALAD

SERVES: 4 • PREPARATION: 10 MINUTES • COOKING: 40 MINUTES

1 pound (500 g) baby beets
5 ounces (150 g) goat's cheese
6 Medjool dates, pitted
7 ounces (200 g) baby arugula
⅓ cup (75 ml) walnuts

DRESSING:
3 tablespoons (45 ml) extra virgin oil
1 garlic clove, chopped
2 tablespoons (30 ml) white wine vinegar
2 teaspoons (10 ml) honey

1 2
3 4

1	Preheat oven to 400°F (200°C). Put the beets into a roasting pan and bake for 40 minutes, or until soft.	2	Cut the beets into wedges and slice the goat's cheese and dates.
3	To make the dressing, whisk together the oil, garlic, vinegar and honey in a bowl.	4	Arrange the beets, goat's cheese, dates and arugula on a plate, drizzle the dressing over the salad and sprinkle the walnuts on top.

SEVEN-VEGETABLE TAGINE

❧ SERVES: 4 • PREPARATION: 20 MINUTES • COOKING: 40 MINUTES ❧

2 tablespoons (30 ml) olive oil
2 medium onions, chopped
½ teaspoon (2 ml) each ground cumin,
   coriander, ginger and cinnamon
¼ teaspoon (1 ml) white pepper
¼ teaspoon (1 ml) turmeric

14 ounces (400 g) large tomatoes, chopped
1 carrot, cut into thick slices
2 zucchini, cut into thick slices
1 small eggplant, halved
10 ounces (300 g) sweet potatoes, cut into
   large pieces

10 ounces (300 g) daikon, cut into thick slices
1 small green pepper, cut into large pieces
¼ cup (60 ml) chopped cilantro
¼ cup (60 ml) chopped parsley
Sea salt and black pepper, to taste
2 cups (500 ml) couscous

1 2
3 4

1	Heat the oil in a large saucepan and fry the onion and spices over medium heat for 10 minutes, or until the onion is soft.	2	Add the tomatoes and 2 cups (500 ml) water. Bring to a boil, then reduce the heat to let simmer.	
3	Add the vegetables, cover and simmer for 20 minutes, or until tender. Stir in the cilantro and parsley and season with salt and pepper.	4	Put the couscous in a bowl, cover with boiling water and allow to stand until the liquid has been absorbed.	➤

5	Fluff the couscous with a fork to separate the grains.	VARIATION ❋
		Try adding dried fruit to the recipe for extra flavor — dried apricots, prunes or raisins would all work well in this dish.

| 6 | Serve the couscous with the vegetable tagine ladled over top. | **VARIATION**
❄
To make a flavored couscous to serve with the tagine, add finely shredded lemon rind, a generous knob of butter and some chopped coriander. |

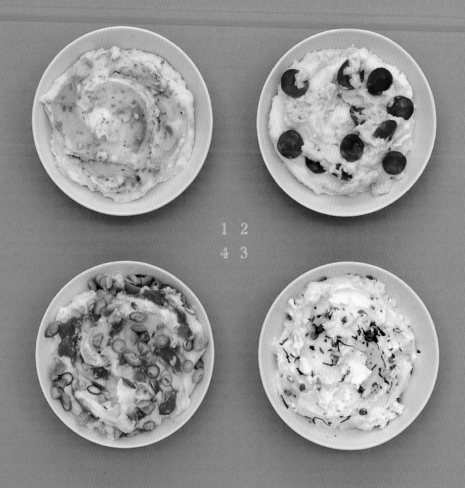

1 2
4 3

POTATO SMASH

✤ SERVES: 4 • PREPARATION: 20 MINUTES • COOKING: 40 MINUTES ✦

FOLLOW STEPS 1 TO 4 FROM METHOD OF RECIPE 1,

1. WASABI & SESAME: Add ¼ teaspoon (1 ml) wasabi, 1 tablespoon (15 ml) soy sauce and 2 teaspoons (10 ml) toasted sesame seeds.

2. CHORIZO & SCRAMBLED EGG: Fry 1 thinly sliced chorizo in a little oil and add it and 2 lightly scrambled eggs to the potatoes.

3. CAPER & CRÈME FRAÎCHE: Stir in 2 tablespoons (30 ml) chopped drained capers, 2 tablespoons (30 ml) crème fraîche or sour cream, 1 tablespoon (15 ml) chopped fresh herbs and zest of 1 lemon.

4. TOMATO & OLIVE: Fry 3½ ounces (100 g) roughly chopped cherry tomatoes in oil, add 2 tablespoons (30 ml) chopped green olives and 2 sliced green onions; add to the puree.

1 2
4 3

PARSNIP MASH

❧ SERVES: 4 • PREPARATION: 20 MINUTES • COOKING: 40 MINUTES ❧

FOLLOW STEPS 1 TO 4 FROM METHOD OF RECIPE 1, REPLACING THE POTATOES WITH PARSNIPS.

1. HARISSA YOGURT: Mix in 1 teaspoon (5 ml) harissa, 2 tablespoons (30 ml) Greek yogurt and 1 tablespoon (15 ml) chopped coriander.

2. MANCHEGO & MEMBRILLO: Finely grate 1¾ ounces (50 g) Manchego, beat in 1 tablespoon (15 ml) roughly chopped dulce de membrillo (quince paste) and add to the parsnips.

3. PINK PEPPERCORN: Stir in 2 teaspoons (10 ml) lightly crushed pink peppercorns, 1 tablespoon (15 ml) snipped chives and 2 tablespoons (30 ml) caramelized onion.

4. HORSERADISH & PARSLEY: Mix in 1 tablespoon (15 ml) hot horseradish, 2 tablespoons (30 ml) fromage frais or low-fat cream cheese and 2 tablespoons (30 ml) chopped parsley.

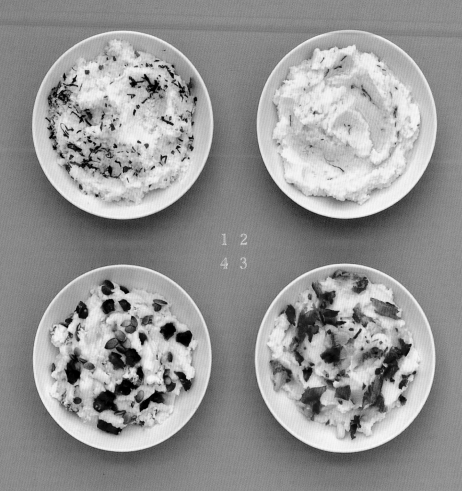

1 2
4 3

CELERIAC PUREE

❧ SERVES: 4 • PREPARATION: 20 MINUTES • COOKING: 40 MINUTES ❧

FOLLOW STEPS 1 TO 4 FROM METHOD OF RECIPE 1, REPLACING THE POTATOES WITH CELERIAC.

1. PARMESAN, PARSLEY & CHILI FLAKE: Finely grate 1¾ ounces (50 g) Parmesan, add zest of 1 lemon, 1 tablespoon (15 ml) chopped parsley and a pinch of chili flakes and beat into puree.

2. SAFFRON & TRUFFLE OIL: Stir through 1 teaspoon (5 ml) saffron threads soaked in 1 tablespoon (15 ml) hot water and drizzle white truffle oil over.

3. ROAST GARLIC & PROSCIUTTO: Roast a head of garlic, peel cloves and mix together with 1 ounce (30 g) prosciutto that was grilled until crisp.

4. BLUE CHEESE, DATE & PUMPKIN SEED: Break 1¾ ounces (50 g) creamy blue cheese into pieces, add 4 chopped fresh dates and 1 tablespoon (15 ml) pumpkin seeds and mix into puree.

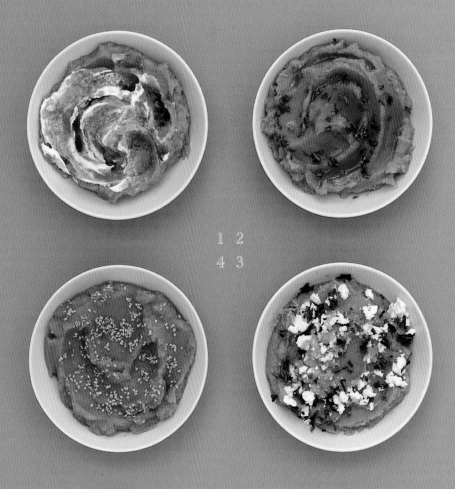

1 2
4 3

SWEET POTATO MASH

❧ SERVES: 4 • PREPARATION: 20 MINUTES • COOKING: 40 MINUTES ❧

FOLLOW STEPS 1 TO 4 FROM METHOD OF RECIPE 1, REPLACING THE POTATOES WITH SWEET POTATOES.

1. CURRY PASTE & YOGURT: Stir in 1 tablespoon (15 ml) toasted sesame seeds, 1 tablespoon (15 ml) honey, 1 tablespoon (15 ml) mild curry paste and 2 tablespoons (30 ml) Greek yogurt.

2. SWEET CHILI SAUCE & CORIANDER: Mix in 2 tablespoons (30 ml) sweet chili sauce, 2 teaspoons (10 ml) lime zest and 2 tablespoons (30 ml) chopped coriander.

3. FETA & MINT: Crumble 3½ ounces (100 g) crumbled feta, add 2 tablespoons (30 ml) chopped mint and 1 teaspoon (5 ml) orange zest and mix into sweet potatoes.

4. SESAME SEED & HONEY: Mix in 1 tablespoon (15 ml) toasted sesame seeds, ½ teaspoon (2 ml) sesame oil and 1 tablespoon (15 ml) honey.

INDIAN VEGETABLE CURRY

❖ SERVES: 4 • PREPARATION: 20 MINUTES • COOKING: 50 MINUTES ❖

2 tablespoons (30 ml) sunflower oil
1 red onion, finely chopped
2 tablespoons (30 ml) Madras curry paste
1 tablespoon (15 ml) grated ginger
2 garlic cloves, finely chopped

1 red pepper, chopped
1 carrot, thickly sliced
10 ounces (300 g) sweet potato, cut into
  cubes
10 ounces (300 g) cauliflower, cut into florets
2 zucchini, sliced

1½ cups (375 ml) fresh or frozen peas
1 (14-fluid ounce/398 ml) can chopped
  tomatoes
5 ounces (150 g) baby spinach
½ cup (125 ml) plain yogurt
¼ cup (60 ml) cashews

1 2
3 4

1	Heat the oil in a saucepan and cook the onion for 10 minutes, or until golden. Add the curry paste, ginger and garlic and cook for 3 minutes.	2	Add the rest of the vegetables, except the spinach, and 1 cup (250 ml) water. Bring to a boil, reduce the heat, cover and simmer for 20 minutes.
3	Remove the lid and simmer uncovered for 15 minutes, or until the vegetables are soft. Remove from the heat and stir in the spinach and yogurt.	4	Sprinkle the cashews on top and serve.

FRUIT-LIKE VEGETABLES

2

......19
...... 20
...... 21
...... 22
......23
...... 24
......25
...... 26
......27
...... 28
...... 29
...... 30
...... 31
......32
.......33

TOMATO PASTA SAUCE

⇒ MAKES:: 1¾ CUPS (400 ML) • PREPARATION: 30 MINUTES • COOKING: 1 MINUTE ⇐

1 pound (500 g) ripe plum tomatoes
10 basil leaves
3 garlic cloves, crushed
3 tablespoons (45 ml) tomato sauce or
  tomato passata
2 tablespoons (30 ml) olive oil

Sea salt and black pepper, to taste

TO SERVE:
Pasta of your choice
Parmesan cheese

NOTE:
You can stir chopped olives,
anchovies, capers, mixed herbs or
seasonings of your choice through the
sauce.

1 2
3 4

1	Put the tomatoes in boiling water for 1 minute, then peel off the skins. Core to remove the seeds and roughly chop the flesh.	2	Put the tomatoes and basil into a food processor and process until smooth.
3	Transfer to a bowl, stir in the garlic, passata or tomato sauce and oil, and season with salt and pepper. Cover and allow to stand for 30 minutes to allow the flavors to combine.	4	Serve tossed through pasta with grated Parmesan cheese, on pizza bases or in a pasta bake.

VEGETABLE LASAGNA

➜ SERVES: 6 • PREPARATION: 40 MINUTES • COOKING: 50 MINUTES ➜

3 tablespoons (45 ml) olive oil
1½ pound (750 g) peeled butternut squash, sliced
2 fennel bulbs, sliced
2 red peppers, cut into thick strips
1¾ ounces (50 g) butter
3 tablespoons (45 ml) all-purpose flour

2½ cups (600 ml) milk
Salt, black pepper and grated nutmeg, to taste
1 onion, finely chopped
2 garlic cloves, crushed
1 celery stick and 1 carrot, chopped
3¼ cups (810 ml) tomato pasta sauce

1 cup (250 ml) dry white wine
1 teaspoon (5 ml) dried oregano
6 fresh lasagna sheets (7 ounces/200 g)
10 ounces (300 g) spinach, wilted
8 ounces (250 g) mozzarella, grated
2 ounces (60 g) Parmesan cheese, grated

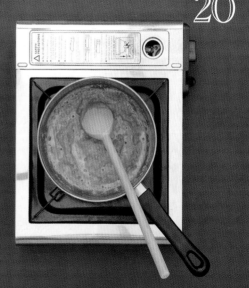

1 2
3 4

1	Preheat oven to 400°F (200°C). Drizzle 2 tablespoons (30 ml) oil over the squash, fennel and pepper and roast for 40 minutes.	2	Make a béchamel sauce by melting the butter in a saucepan, adding the flour and cooking, stirring, until golden.
3	Remove from the heat and stir in the milk. Return to the heat and cook, stirring, until thick. Season with salt, pepper and nutmeg.	4	Heat the remaining oil and fry the onion, garlic, celery and carrot until soft. Add the tomato sauce, wine and oregano. Boil, then simmer covered for 20 minutes. ➢

5 6
7 8

5	Spoon a little of the tomato sauce over the base of a 4-quart (4 L) baking dish and top with a layer of lasagna sheets.	6	Top with a layer of roasted vegetables and then another layer of tomato sauce.
7	Top with another layer of lasagna sheets, the spinach and some of the béchamel sauce.	8	Continue layering the ingredients, finishing with a layer of béchamel sauce. Spread the mozzarella and Parmesan over the top.

 9

Bake for 40 minutes, or until golden, then allow to stand for 10 minutes before serving.

VARIATION
*

For a quicker version of this recipe substitute 2 cups (500 ml) ricotta for the béchamel sauce. Spread it over the spinach as you would the sauce then sprinkle with a little grated nutmeg and season well with salt and pepper.

RATATOUILLE

❖ SERVES: 4 TO 6 • PREPARATION: 20 MINUTES • COOKING: 40 MINUTES ❖

⅔ cup (150 ml) olive oil, plus 2 extra
   tablespoons (30 ml)
1 eggplant, cut into cubes (1 pound/500 g)
1 red pepper, sliced
1 green pepper, sliced

2 zucchini, sliced
2 red onions, cut into wedges
2 garlic cloves, finely chopped
3 ripe tomatoes, peeled and chopped

1 tablespoon (15 ml) chopped parsley
1 tablespoon (15 ml) chopped thyme
Sea salt and black pepper, to taste

1 2
3 4

1	Heat the oil in a frying pan and cook the eggplant in batches until golden. Drain in a sieve set over a bowl to catch the excess oil.	2	Add 2 tablespoons (30 ml) of oil to the pan and cook the peppers until soft. Add the zucchini and cook until golden. Transfer to the sieve.
3	Add the excess oil to the pan and fry the onions for 5 minutes. Fry the garlic for 5 minutes. Add the tomatoes; bring to a boil, then simmer for 10 minutes.	4	Return all the vegetables to the pan, add the herbs and cook for 5 minutes. Season with salt and pepper and serve.

GAZPACHO

❖ SERVES: 4 TO 6 • PREPARATION: 20 MINUTES • COOKING: NONE ❖

1¾ ounces (50 g) crusty stale bread,
  sliced
2¼ pounds (1 kg) ripe tomatoes, quartered
1 green onion, chopped

2 garlic cloves, finely chopped
1 green pepper, chopped
1 cucumber, peeled, deseeded and
  chopped

1 tablespoon (15 ml) red wine vinegar
¼ cup (60 ml) extra virgin olive oil
Sea salt and black pepper, to taste
Mint leaves, to garnish

1 2
3 4

1	Tear the bread into pieces and soak in a bowl of cold water for 15 minutes, or until soft.	2	Drain the bread and transfer to a blender; add the tomatoes, onion, garlic and most of the pepper and cucumber, reserving a little for the garnish.
3	Blend until smooth, add the vinegar, half the olive oil and season with salt and pepper.	4	Serve the gazpacho topped with the reserved chopped pepper and cucumber, the remaining oil and the mint.

MINESTRONE SOUP

⇻ SERVES: 4 • PREPARATION: 30 MINUTES • COOKING: 1 HOUR ⇺

1 cup (250 ml) dry romano beans
2 tablespoons (30 ml) olive oil
1 onion, chopped
1 garlic clove, finely chopped
3½ ounces (100 g) pancetta, chopped
2 celery sticks, chopped

2 carrots, chopped
1 potato, chopped
1 zucchini, chopped
5 ounces (150 g) green beans, chopped
5 ripe tomatoes, chopped
1 tablespoon (15 ml) tomato puree

8 cups (2 L) chicken stock
1 bay leaf
1 cup (250 ml) small pasta
3½ ounces (100 g) Chinese cabbage, shredded
Sea salt and black pepper, to taste
4 tablespoons (60 ml) pesto

1	Soak the Romano beans in cold water 10 to 12 hours, then rinse and drain.	2	Boil in a large pan until tender. Leave in the cooking liquid until ready to add to the soup, then drain.	
3	Heat the oil in a large saucepan and cook the onion, garlic and pancetta for 10 minutes, or until the onions are soft and the pancetta is golden.	4	Add the celery, carrot, potato, zucchini and green beans and cook for a further 5 minutes, or until the vegetables soften.	➤

5 Add the tomatoes, tomato puree, stock and bay leaf. Bring to a boil, then reduce the heat and simmer for 30 minutes. Stir in the pasta, cabbage and drained Romano beans and cook for a further 10 minutes.

TIP

Add the rind from a piece of Parmesan cheese when you add the liquid in step 5; it will help flavor the stock as the soup cooks.

6 Season with salt and pepper, then serve bowls of the minestrone topped with pesto.

VARIATION
❋

For a vegetarian version omit the pancetta and use vegetable stock instead of chicken stock. For extra richness, you may like to add some chopped sun-dried tomatoes.

PANZANELLA

❧ SERVES:: 4 • PREPARATION: 20 MINUTES • COOKING: 15 MINUTES ❧

1 red pepper
1 yellow pepper
1½ pounds (750 g) ripe tomatoes, chopped
Sea salt, to taste
1 stale country loaf (8 ounces/250 g)

⅓ cup (75 ml) olive oil
2 tablespoons (30 ml) red wine vinegar
2 garlic cloves, crushed
3½ ounces (100 g) sun-dried tomatoes,
  chopped
1 celery heart, sliced

1 tablespoon (15 ml) capers
½ cup (250 ml) roughly torn basil leaves
Grated Parmesan cheese, to serve

1 2
3 4

1	Grill or broil the peppers and peel off the skins (see recipe 25), cut flesh into strips. Put the tomatoes in a sieve over a bowl, sprinkle salt over and leave for 20 minutes.	2	Tear the bread into bite-sized pieces and put in a bowl.
3	Whisk together the tomato juice from the draining bowl, olive oil, vinegar and garlic.	4	Put the tomatoes, peppers, bread and the rest of the ingredients in a bowl. Mix in the dressing and leave for 10 minutes. Serve with Parmesan.

CHARGRILLED PEPPERS

❧ SERVES: 4 • PREPARATION: 15 MINUTES • COOKING: 20 MINUTES ❧

1 red pepper
1 green pepper
1 yellow pepper
8 slices ciabatta
1 garlic clove, halved

2 tablespoons (30 ml) olive oil, plus extra
  to drizzle
2 tablespoons (30 ml) shredded basil
1 tablespoon (15 ml) balsamic vinegar

NOTE:
The chargrilled peppers may be stored in an airtight container in the refrigerator. They are delicious served on an antipasto platter with cheeses and cold meats.

1
4

2
5

3
6

1	Broil the peppers on a baking sheet in a hot oven until the skins blister and blacken.	2	Transfer the peppers to a plastic bag and set aside to cool.	3	Once cool, peel away the skin and cut the flesh into thin strips.
4	Toast the bread and rub with the halved garlic and drizzle with olive oil.	5	Put the peppers in a bowl and add the basil, oil and vinegar; mix well.	6	Top the toast with the peppers and serve.

ZUCCHINI FRITTERS

❧ SERVES: 4 (MAKES 12) • PREPARATION: 20 MINUTES • COOKING: 30 MINUTES ❧

12 ounces (350 g) zucchini
Sea salt, to taste
1 cup (250 ml) chickpea flour or brown
  rice flour
1 teaspoon (5 ml) ground cumin
1 teaspoon (5 ml) allspice

¼ teaspoon baking soda
3 tablespoons (45 ml) chopped cilantro
3 tablespoons (45 ml) chopped mint
2 tablespoons (30 ml) chopped dill
3 green onions, sliced

5 ounces (150 g) feta cheese, crumbled
  (about 1¼ cups/310 ml)
¼ cup (60 ml) olive oil
6 radishes, finely sliced
1 small orange, segmented
¼ red onion, finely sliced

1 2
3 4

1	Grate the zucchini, sprinkle salt over them and let stand for 20 minutes.	2	Squeeze out any excess moisture from the zucchini.	
3	Whisk together the flour, cumin, allspice, baking soda and ¾ cup (175 ml) water to make a thick batter.	4	Add the zucchini, herbs, green onions and feta and mix gently to combine.	➢

| 5 | Heat 3 tablespoons (45 ml) of oil in a large frying pan, add 2 tablespoons (30 ml) of the batter and cook for 2 minutes, or until golden. Flip and cook the other side. Keep warm while you cook the remaining batter. | **NOTE**
❋
These fritters make excellent picnic food and are perfect served hot or cold. You may like to vary the salad you serve them with — a simple chopped tomato, red onion and mint salad is a lovely alternative. |

		VARIATION
6	Combine the radishes, orange and onion and serve on top of the fritters.	You can use grated carrot or parsnip instead of the grated zucchini.

BABA GHANOUSH

❧ SERVES: 4 • PREPARATION: 15 MINUTES • COOKING: 1 HOUR ❧

1 medium eggplant (about 1 pound/500 g)
1 tablespoon (15 ml) lemon juice
2 garlic cloves, crushed
Sea salt, to taste
1 tablespoon (15 ml) tahini

TO SERVE:

Paprika
Extra virgin olive oil
Pita bread, cut into triangles

1 2
3 4

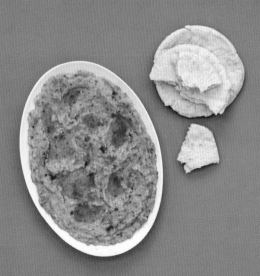

1	Preheat oven to 400°F (200°C) and bake the eggplant for 1 hour. Transfer to a bag, allow to cool for 15 minutes, then peel off the skin.	2	Roughly chop the eggplant flesh and transfer to a bowl. Add the lemon juice, garlic, salt and tahini and mix to combine.
3	Blend the mixture until smooth, then spoon onto a plate and spread it into an even layer.	4	Top with paprika and olive oil and serve with pita bread.

EGGPLANT PARMIGIANA

⇻ SERVES: 4 TO 6 • PREPARATION: 1 HOUR • COOKING: 1 HOUR ⇺

1 onion, finely chopped
2 garlic cloves, finely chopped
1 tablespoon (15 ml) olive oil, plus extra for
 shallow-frying
1 (14 ounce/398 ml) can chopped tomatoes
½ cup (125 ml) white wine

2 tablespoons (30 ml) chopped basil
1 pound (500 g) eggplant
3 cups (750 ml) fresh bread crumbs
1½ teaspoons (7 ml) dried Italian herbs
⅔ cup (150 ml) grated pecorino cheese
All-purpose flour, for dusting

3 eggs

TOPPING:
1 cup (250 ml) grated pecorino cheese
7 ounces (200 g) mozzarella cheese, sliced

1 2
3 4

1	Preheat oven to 350°F (180°C). Fry the onion and the garlic in the oil. Add the tomatoes and wine. Bring to a boil then simmer for 20 minutes. Stir in the basil.	2	Peel the eggplant and cut into long, thin slices.
3	Combine the bread crumbs, herbs and cheese. Put the flour and egg in separate bowls. Coat the eggplant in flour first, then in eggs, then the bread crumbs.	4	Shallow-fry the eggplant in batches in a large frying pan until crisp and golden brown. Drain on paper towels. ➤

5   Spoon a little of the tomato sauce into the base of a 4-quart (4 L) baking dish, top with a layer of eggplant and sprinkle the pecorino cheese over. Continue layering until you have used all of the ingredients.

NOTE
❊

It is very important that you slice the eggplant thinly, if it is cut too thickly it will not cook through, and it will make the crumb coating soggy.

6

Finish with a layer of sliced mozzarella and bake for 40 minutes, or until the top is golden. Serve with salad.

VARIATION

Serve individual dishes of eggplant parmigiana in shallow baking dishes. The cooked dish also freezes very well.

BUTTERNUT SQUASH SOUP

❧ SERVES: 4 • PREPARATION: 20 MINUTES • COOKING: 50 MINUTES ❧

1½ pounds (750 g) butternut squash,
  peeled and cut into wedges
1 red onion, cut into large wedges
1 head garlic
3 rosemary sprigs
1 tablespoon (15 ml) olive oil

4 cups (1 L) chicken stock
Sea salt and black pepper, to taste
Grated nutmeg, to taste
½ cup (125 ml) crème fraîche or sour cream
2 tablespoons (30 ml) snipped chives

NOTE:
You can add flavorings to this basic soup
recipe. Add 1 tablespoon (15 ml) red curry
paste or 1 tablespoon (15 ml) of grated
ginger.

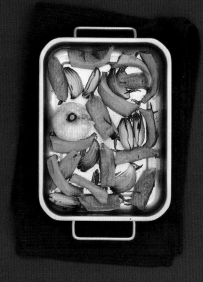

1 2
3 4

1	Preheat oven to 400°F (200°C). Put the squash, onion, garlic and rosemary in a roasting pan, drizzle oil over and bake until soft.	2	Peel the garlic. Remove and discard the rosemary from the roasting pan.
3	Put the squash, onion and garlic in a saucepan, add stock and bring to a boil. Reduce heat and cook for 15 minutes. Blend in a blender until smooth.	4	Season the soup with salt, pepper and nutmeg and serve in bowls with a spoonful of crème fraîche or sour cream and a few snipped chives.

BUTTERNUT SQUASH RAVIOLI

➤ SERVES: 4 • PREPARATION: 40 MINUTES • COOKING: 10 MINUTES ◆

14 ounces (400 g) butternut squash, peeled
  and chopped
⅔ cup (150 ml) ricotta cheese
2 tablespoons (30 ml) toasted pine nuts
1 tablespoon (15 ml) chopped thyme

1 teaspoon (5 ml) grated lemon zest
10 ounces (300 g) wonton wrappers
½ cup (125 ml) butter
1 tablespoon (15 ml) sage leaves

1 2
3 4

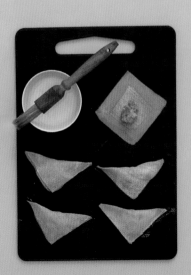

1	Preheat oven to 400°F (200°C). Put the squash on a baking sheet and bake for 30 minutes, or until soft.	2	Transfer to a bowl, add the ricotta, pine nuts, thyme and lemon zest and mix to combine. Season with salt and pepper.	
3	Place a wrapper on a hard surface, put a heaped teaspoon of the filling in the center, fold into a triangle and seal (see note).	4	Melt the butter in a frying pan until nutty brown, add the sage leaves and cook until softened.	➤

5 Boil the ravioli in batches in a large pot of lightly salted water for 2 to 3 minutes, or until they float to the surface. Remove with a slotted spoon and put on a baking sheet lined with parchment paper while you cook the remaining ravioli.

NOTE
❄

At step 3, brush the edges of the wonton wrapper with water then fold into a triangle and gently press the edges to seal.

	Serve the ravioli in shallow bowls with the sage butter drizzled over top.	
6		The filling can also be used to make cannelloni; simply spoon the filling along the end of fresh lasagna sheets and follow the method used in recipe 60.

GUACAMOLE

❖ SERVES: 6 • PREPARATION: 10 MINUTES • COOKING: NONE ❖

2 ripe avocados
1 tablespoon (15 ml) lime juice
1 garlic clove, crushed
Dash of Tabasco sauce

½ small red onion, finely chopped
1 small tomato, diced
Sea salt and black pepper, to taste
Corn chips, to serve

1 2
3 4

1	Cut the avocados in half and carefully remove the pits.	2	Mash the avocado and lime juice together until smooth and creamy.
3	Add the garlic, Tabasco, red onion and tomato and mix to combine.	4	Season with salt and pepper and serve with corn chips.

TZATZIKI

❖ SERVES: 4 • PREPARATION: 10 MINUTES • COOKING: NONE ❖

½ cucumber
2 tablespoons (30 ml) mint leaves
1 garlic clove
2 cups (500 ml) Greek-style yogurt

Sea salt, to taste
1 tablespoon (15 ml) lemon juice
1 teaspoon (5 ml) dried mint

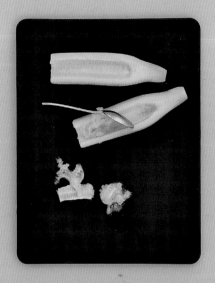

1 2
3 4

1	Peel the cucumber and remove the seeds using a spoon.	2	Finely chop the cucumber, fresh mint and garlic. Put the cucumber in a sieve over a bowl and press out the excess moisture.
3	Transfer the cucumber to a bowl, add the yogurt, garlic, salt, lemon juice and the fresh and dried mint and mix well to combine.	4	Serve with crudités.

STUFFED PEPPERS

❧ SERVES: 4 • PREPARATION: 20 MINUTES • COOKING: 30 TO 40 MINUTES ❧

1 yellow pepper
1 green pepper
1 red pepper
3 ripe Roma tomatoes, quartered

4 marinated artichoke hearts, quartered
2 garlic cloves, sliced
3½ ounces (100 g) Kalamata olives, pitted
8 caperberries

3½ ounces (100 g) feta cheese, crumbled,
   about ¾ cup/175 ml)
Extra virgin olive oil
3 basil leaves, torn

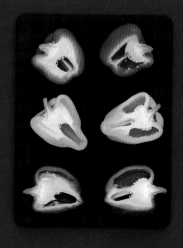

1 2
3 4

1	Preheat oven to 375°F (190°C). Cut the peppers in half.	2	Remove the cores and white veins from the inside of the peppers.
3	Put the peppers on a baking sheet. Fill the peppers with the tomato, artichokes, garlic, olives, caperberries and feta.	4	Drizzle the oil over and bake for about 30 to 40 minutes, until soft and golden. Sprinkle basil over and serve.

CABBAGE

3

Cabbage Rolls 34
Cabbage & Pork Pot Stickers 35
Cauliflower with Cheese 36
Sprouts with Pancetta 37
Stir-fried Broccoli & Kale 38

CABBAGE ROLLS

❧ SERVES: 6 • PREPARATION: 40 MINUTES • COOKING: 1 1/2 HOURS ❧

2¼ pounds (1 kg) green cabbage
1 onion, peeled
1 pound (500 g) ground beef
⅓ cup (75 ml) long-grain rice, rinsed
1 onion, grated
2 garlic cloves, crushed

1½ teaspoons (7 ml) allspice
½ teaspoon (2 ml) paprika
2 tablespoons (30 ml) chopped parsley
Sea salt and cracked black pepper, to taste
SAUCE:
4 garlic cloves, minced with salt

1 tablespoon (15 ml) dried mint
3 tablespoons (45 ml) butter, chopped
1¾ pounds (800 g) chopped peeled
    tomatoes
2 to 4 cups (500 ml to 1 L) chicken stock
1 cup (250 ml) white wine

1 2
3 4

1	Remove the core from the cabbage.	2	Boil the cabbage and the peeled onion until soft. Let cool.	
3	Mix the meat, rice, grated onion, garlic, spices and parsley to combine. Season with salt and pepper.	4	Separate the cabbage leaves and trim the thick vein. Put 2 tablespoons (30 ml) of the meat mixture on top of a leaf.	➤

5 6
7 8

5	Roll up to enclose the filling, tucking in the edges as you go.	6	Line the base of a saucepan with cabbage leaves. Top with a layer of filled leaves.
7	Top with some garlic, dried mint, butter and tomatoes.	8	Continue layering until you have used up all of the ingredients. Pour over the chicken stock and wine. Weight down with a plate.

9 | Cover and cook over medium heat for 50 minutes. Remove from the heat and allow to rest for 30 minutes before serving.

VARIATION
❊

You can vary the meat you use for this recipe, such as pork or lamb. Try adding other dried herbs, like oregano, thyme and rosemary, but use sparingly, as you don't want their flavor to overpower the subtle flavor of the rolls. This dish will richen over time, so it is best if made a day ahead of serving.

CABBAGE & PORK POT STICKERS

❧ MAKES: 30 • PREPARATION: 30 MINUTES • COOKING: 15 MINUTES ❧

8 ounces (250 g) ground pork
1 cup (250 ml) cooked shredded Chinese
  cabbage, well drained
2 green onions, sliced
1 tablespoon (15 ml) grated ginger
1 tablespoon (15 ml) soy sauce

2 teaspoons (10 ml) mirin
2 teaspoons (10 ml) sake
1 to 2 teaspoons (5 to 10 ml) cornstarch
¼ teaspoon (1 ml) sesame oil
30 pot-sticker wrappers, or as needed
2 tablespoons (30 ml) vegetable oil, for frying

DIPPING SAUCE:

2 tablespoons (30 ml) soy sauce
2 tablespoons (30 ml) rice vinegar

1 2
3 4

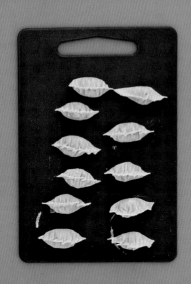

1	Put the pork, cabbage, green onions, ginger, soy sauce, mirin, sake, cornstarch and sesame oil in a bowl and mix to combine.	2	Lay the pot-sticker wrappers on a cutting board and place 2 teaspoons (10 ml) of filling into the center of each wrapper.	
3	Brush the edges of the wrappers lightly with water and pinch the edges together to seal.	4	Heat the oil in a frying pan, add enough pot stickers to cover the base of the pan and cook until the bottoms are crisp.	➤

| 5 | Add 1½ cups (125 ml) water, cover and cook for 5 minutes, or until all of the liquid has evaporated. | **VARIATION**
❋
You can substitute the ground pork with ground chicken, flaked fish, shrimps or well-drained tofu. |

		NOTE
		❋
	Mix the soy sauce and rice vinegar together in a small bowl and serve with the pot stickers.	Pot stickers can be made ahead of time and frozen uncooked. Thaw before cooking.
6		

CAULIFLOWER WITH CHEESE

SERVES: 4 • PREPARATION: 20 MINUTES • COOKING: 30 MINUTES

2¼ pounds (1 kg) cauliflower
3 tablespoons (45 ml) butter
3 tablespoons (45 ml) all-purpose flour
2½ cups (625 ml) milk
2 teaspoons (10 ml) Dijon mustard
1 cup (250 ml) grated Emmentaler or Cheddar cheese
Sea salt and black pepper, to taste

1	Preheat oven to 425°F (220°C). Cut the cauliflower into large florets and steam until tender.	2	Make a sauce with butter, flour and milk (see recipe 20). When thick, add the mustard and half the cheese and cook for 5 minutes. Season with salt and pepper.
3	Arrange the cauliflower in a 1½-quart (1½ L) baking dish and pour the sauce over. Sprinkle the remaining cheese on top.	4	Bake for 15 minutes, or until the sauce is bubbling and golden, then serve.

SPROUTS WITH PANCETTA

✈ SERVES: 4 • PREPARATION: 15 MINUTES • COOKING: 30 MINUTES ✈

1 pound (500 g) Brussels sprouts
1 tablespoon (15 ml) olive oil
2 tablespoons (30 ml) butter
3½ ounces (100 g) pancetta, chopped

7½ ounces (220 g) chestnuts, roasted and
   peeled or 1 (7-ounce/200 g) can chestnuts
Sea salt and cracked black pepper, to taste

1 2
3 4

1	Cut the Brussels sprouts in half and remove any old outer leaves.	2	Boil in a pot of lightly salted water for 5 minutes.
3	Heat the oil and butter in a frying pan and cook the pancetta until slightly crisp.	4	Add the Brussels sprouts and chestnuts to the pan and cook until heated through. Season with salt and pepper and serve.

STIR-FRIED BROCCOLI & KALE

❧ SERVES: 4 • PREPARATION: 10 MINUTES • COOKING: 15 MINUTES ❧

3½ ounces (100 g) kale
2 tablespoons (30 ml) pine nuts
1¾ ounces (50 g) butter
1½ tablespoons (22 ml) olive oil
2 garlic cloves, finely chopped

½ teaspoon (2 ml) chili flakes
3 anchovies, roughly chopped
2 bunches purple sprouting broccoli, or
  other variety of broccoli, trimmed

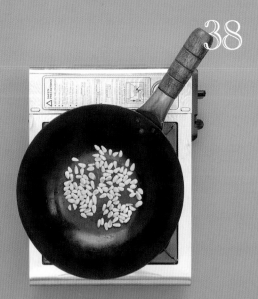

1 2
3 4

1	Put the kale in a bowl and pour boiling water over it. Leave until soft.	2	Toast the pine nuts in a dry wok. Remove and set aside.
3	Heat the butter and oil in the wok and fry the garlic, chili and anchovies until the garlic is golden. Add the broccoli and kale and 3 tablespoons (45 ml) water.	4	Stir-fry until the broccoli is bright green and tender. Sprinkle the pine nuts over and serve.

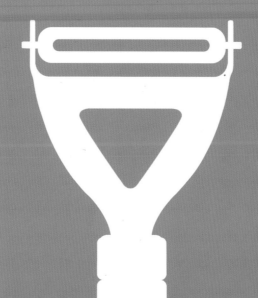

STALKS, SHOOTS
& THISTLES

4

Asparagus with Hollandaise 39
Artichokes with Vinaigrette 40
Slow-cooked Fennel 41
Fennel & Parmesan Salad 42

ASPARAGUS WITH HOLLANDAISE

❖ SERVES: 4 TO 6 • PREPARATION: 15 MINUTES • COOKING: 20 MINUTES ❖

3 egg yolks
¾ cup (175 ml) butter, chopped
2 teaspoons (10 ml) lemon juice

Sea salt and black pepper, to taste
2 bunches asparagus

1 2
3 4

1	Whisk the egg yolks and 2 tablespoons (30 ml) water in a heat-proof bowl. Set the bowl over a pot of simmering water and add a little butter.	2	Add butter a little at a time, allowing it to melt before you add more, then whisk over low heat until thick. Stir in lemon juice and season.
3	Blanch the asparagus in a frying pan of lightly salted water.	4	Serve the asparagus topped with the hollandaise sauce.

ARTICHOKES WITH VINAIGRETTE

✦ SERVES: 4 • PREPARATION: 20 MINUTES • COOKING: 20 MINUTES ✦

1 tablespoon (15 ml) lemon juice
4 globe artichokes

DRESSING:
2 tablespoons (30 ml) white wine vinegar
1 tablespoon (15 ml) lemon juice
1 tablespoon (15 ml) Dijon mustard
1 garlic clove, finely chopped

1 tablespoon (15 ml) chopped fresh herbs,
  such as parsley, chives and tarragon
⅓ cup (75 ml) extra virgin olive oil

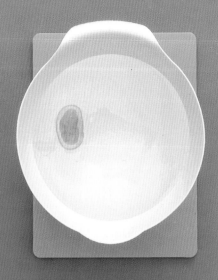

1 2
3 4

1	Put the lemon juice in a bowl of water large enough to hold the artichokes.	2	Remove the stalk from each artichoke and use a vegetable peeler to trim any remaining stalk from the base of the artichokes.	
3	Break off any tough outer leaves, and cut the top off each artichoke.	4	Boil the artichokes until soft. When ready, a leaf will pull away easily from the heart.	➤

	To make the dressing, whisk together the vinegar, lemon juice, mustard, garlic, herbs and olive oil.	**NOTE** ❋
5		When you get to the center of the artichoke, use a spoon to remove the hairy choke and eat the heart.

6 | Serve the artichokes with the dressing. Dip the leaves in the dressing and eat the fleshy base of the leaf.

VARIATION
❁

Serve the artichokes with any dressing , such as those described in recipes 57a and 57b. Enjoy the artichokes hot or cold.

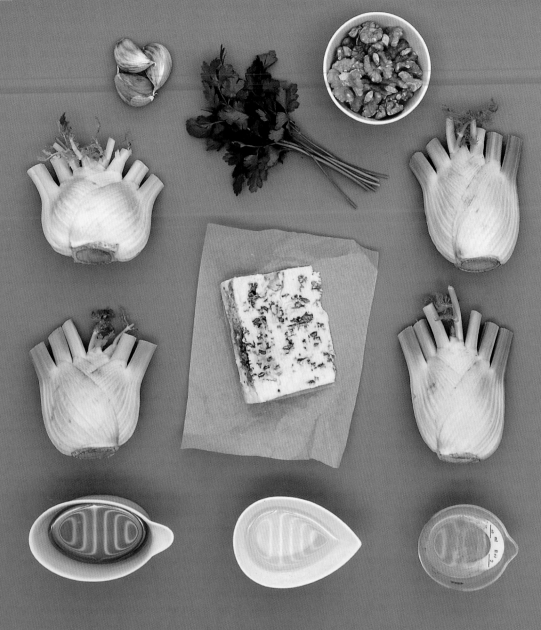

SLOW-COOKED FENNEL

❖ SERVES: 4 • PREPARATION: 15 MINUTES • COOKING: 40 MINUTES ❖

2 medium or 4 small fennel bulbs, trimmed
1 tablespoon (15 ml) olive oil
½ cup (125 ml) white wine
3 garlic cloves, finely chopped

¼ cup (60 ml) chicken stock
3½ ounces (100 g) blue cheese, crumbled
   (about ¾ cup/175 ml)
1¾ ounces (50 g) walnuts, roughly chopped

2 tablespoons (30 ml) parsley leaves
Sea salt and black pepper, to taste

1 2
3 4

1	Boil the fennel in salted water for 20 minutes, then drain and set aside for 10 minutes. Cut into thick slices.	2	Heat the oil in a frying pan and brown the fennel in batches.
3	Add the wine, ¼ cup (60 ml) water, garlic and stock, cover and simmer for 10 minutes.	4	Remove from the heat, sprinkle the cheese, walnuts and parsley over and season with salt and pepper.

FENNEL & PARMESAN SALAD

❧ SERVES: 4 • PREPARATION: 20 MINUTES • COOKING: NONE ❧

2 oranges
2 lemons
4 small fennel bulbs with fronds
1 teaspoon (5 ml) Dijon mustard

¼ cup (60 ml) extra virgin olive oil
1¾ ounces (75 g) Parmesan cheese
1¾ ounces (75 g) flaked almonds, toasted

1 2
3 4

1	Shave half of the Parmesan and grate the other half. Segment one of the oranges.	2	Finely grate the rind of the other orange and of one lemon, then squeeze the juice from the orange and lemon. Thinly slice the fennel.
3	Whisk the lemon juice, orange juice, mustard and oil together in a small bowl.	4	Put the fennel, fronds and orange pieces on plates. Sprinkle the grated rinds, Parmesan and dressing over. Add the almonds and serve.

MUSHROOMS

5

Chargrilled Mushrooms 43

Creamy Mushroom Sauce 44

Mushroom Omelet 45

Wild Mushroom Risotto 46

Mushroom Soup 47

Mushroom Toasts 48

Mushroom Yakitori 49

CHARGRILLED MUSHROOMS

❧ SERVES: 4 • PREPARATION: 10 MINUTES • COOKING: 10 MINUTES ❧

4 large portobellos or white mushrooms
1¾ ounces (50 g) butter, softened
2 garlic cloves, finely chopped

2 tablespoons (30 ml) chopped herbs, such
as parsley, oregano and chives
Cracked black pepper, to taste

1 tablespoon (15 ml) olive oil
1 tablespoon (15 ml) balsamic vinegar

1 2
3 4

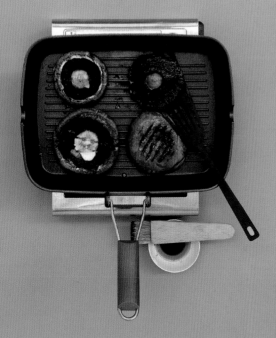

1	Remove the stalks from the mushrooms and brush the caps to remove any dirt.	2	Put the butter, garlic, herbs and pepper in a bowl and beat to combine.
3	Combine the oil and vinegar and brush on the mushrooms. Cook on a barbecue or grill pan for 5 to 10 minutes until soft and golden.	4	Serve the mushrooms topped with a knob of the herb butter.

CREAMY MUSHROOM SAUCE

→ SERVES: 4 • PREPARATION: 10 MINUTES • COOKING: 25 MINUTES ←

¼ ounce (10 g) dried porcini mushrooms
1 tablespoon (15 ml) olive oil
4 green onions, sliced
2 garlic cloves, crushed

7 ounces (200 g) prosciutto, chopped
10 ounces (300 g) chestnut mushrooms, sliced
1 cup (250 ml) dry white wine
1¼ cups (310 ml) light cream (20%)

½ cup (125ml) chicken stock
2 tablespoons (30 ml) chopped parsley
Sea salt and black pepper, to taste
10 ounces (300 g) fettuccine

1 2
3 4

1	Soak the porcini mushrooms in ½ cup (125 ml) boiling water for 15 minutes, or until soft.	2	Heat the oil in a frying pan and cook the green onions and garlic over medium heat for 3 minutes, or until the green onions are soft.	
3	Add the prosciutto and fresh mushrooms and fry for 5 minutes, or until the mushrooms brown.	4	Stir in the wine, scraping the bottom of the pan to deglaze. Boil until nearly evaporated.	➤

		NOTE
5	Add the cream, stock and porcini mushrooms with their soaking liquid, then bring back to a boil and cook for 5 minutes, or until thickened slightly. Stir in the parsley and season with salt and pepper.	A skin will form on the sauce if it is left to sit uncovered for too long, so if you are making the sauce ahead of time, place a piece of greased parchment paper over the surface to prevent this.

6	Boil the pasta in a large pot of salted water until al dente, then drain. Add to the sauce and cook gently until the sauce coats the pasta. Serve.	**VARIATION** ✳ Try using brandy or Marsala in the cream sauce instead of white wine, making sure you bring it to a boil to cook off the alcohol, as you do with the wine.

MUSHROOM OMELET

❧ SERVES: 1 • PREPARATION: 15 MINUTES • COOKING: 10 MINUTES ❧

1¼ ounces (40 g) butter
5 ounces (150 g) crimini mushrooms, sliced
1 garlic clove, finely chopped
2 eggs

1 tablespoon (15 ml) chopped parsley
1 tablespoon (15 ml) chopped chives
Sea salt and black pepper, to taste

2 tablespoons (30 ml) finely grated
Parmesan cheese

1 2
3 4

1	Melt 1 ounce (30 g) butter, add the mushrooms and garlic and cook for 10 minutes, or until the moisture is evaporated. Remove from the heat.	2	Whisk the eggs, herbs, salt and pepper together. Melt the remaining butter, then the egg mixture.
3	Stir the eggs in the pan until they start to set. Top one half with the mushrooms and Parmesan.	4	Gently fold the other half of the omelet onto the mushrooms, remove from the pan and serve immediately.

WILD MUSHROOM RISOTTO

❧ SERVES: 4 • PREPARATION: 20 MINUTES • COOKING: 50 MINUTES ❧

¼ ounce (10 g) dried porcini mushrooms
6 cups (1.5 L) chicken stock
½ cup (125 ml) white wine
1 tablespoon (15 ml) olive oil
1¾ ounces (50 g) butter
1 leek, sliced

2 garlic cloves, finely chopped
2 cups (500 ml) arborio rice
7 ounces (200 g) crimini mushrooms, sliced
7 ounces (200 g) small portobello mushrooms, sliced
1¾ ounces (50 g) Parmesan cheese

3 tablespoons (45 ml) mascarpone cheese
4 ounces (125 g) oyster mushroms
Sea salt and black pepper, to taste
2 cups (500 ml) dried bread crumbs
Vegetable oil, for shallow-frying
Lemon wedges, to serve (optional)

1 2
3 4

1	Put the porcini, stock and wine into a saucepan, then bring to a boil to cook off the alcohol. Reduce the heat to a slow simmer.	2	Heat the oil and butter in a saucepan and cook the leek until soft. Add the garlic and cook for 1 minute. Add the rice and cook for 3 minutes.	
3	Add all the mushrooms except the oyster and cook until soft. Stir in 1 cup (250 ml) of the stock mixture and cook until the liquid is absorbed.	4	Continue to add the stock until the rice is tender. Off the heat, stir in the cheeses and oyster mushrooms. Season with salt and pepper.	➤

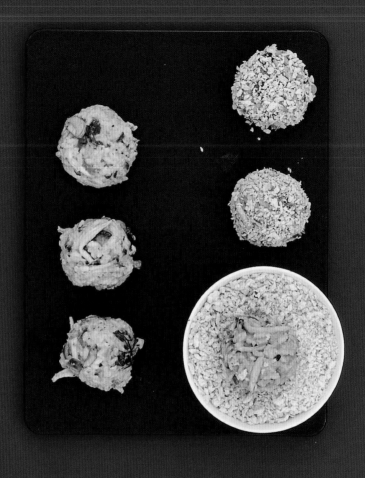

5	If you would like to make risotto cakes, allow the risotto to cool, then shape 2 tablespoons (30 ml) of the mixture into a patty and roll in bread crumbs. Repeat with the rest of the mixture.

NOTES
✻

In step 4, gradually add ½ cup (125 ml) at a time, waiting for it to be completely absorbed before adding more, until all of the liquid has been used and the rice is tender. The rice should be slightly soupy.

If you are making the risotto cakes omit the mascarpone cheese or the cakes will be too soft.

| 6 | Working in batches, shallow-fry the patties in a frying pan until crisp and golden and heated through. Serve with lemon wedges. | **VARIATION**
❋
You can put a filling in the center of the patties — try a cube of mozzarella with some chopped fried onions. |

MUSHROOM SOUP

➤ SERVES: 4 • PREPARATION: 20 MINUTES • COOKING: 30 MINUTES ◆

1 tablespoon (15 ml) olive oil
1¾ ounces (50 g) butter
1 leek, sliced
2 garlic cloves, finely chopped

1 pound (500 g) large portobello or white
  mushrooms, wiped, stalks removed and
  caps sliced
2 teaspoons (10 ml) all-purpose flour

4 cups (1 L) chicken stock
1 cup (250 ml) light or half-and-half cream
Sea salt and black pepper, to taste

1 2
3 4

1	Heat the oil and butter in a saucepan. Cook the leek until golden. Add garlic and cook for 1 minute. Add the mushrooms and cook until soft.	2	Remove ½ cup (125 ml) of the mushrooms and set aside as a garnish for the soup. Add the flour to the pan and cook, stirring, for 2 minutes.
3	Add the stock and bring to a boil. Reduce the heat and simmer for 10 minutes. Stir in the cream. Puree in a blender or food processor then reheat gently.	4	Season with salt and pepper, transfer to serving bowls and finish with the reserved mushrooms.

MUSHROOM TOASTS

➤ SERVES: 4 • PREPARATION: 15 MINUTES • COOKING: 25 MINUTES ➤

1 tablespoon (15 ml) olive oil
1¾ ounces (15 ml) butter
2 shallots, finely chopped
2 garlic cloves, finely chopped
1 pound (500 g) mixed mushrooms,
  chopped

3 thyme sprigs
1 cup (250 ml) white wine

TOASTS:
4 thick slices ciabatta
1 tablespoon (15 ml) olive oil
2 garlic cloves, halved
3½ ounces (100 g) Gorgonzola cheese
1 tablespoon (15 ml) snipped chives

1 2
3 4

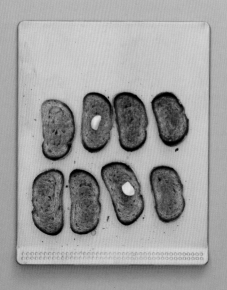

1	Heat the oil and butter and cook the shallots and chopped garlic until golden. Add the mushrooms and thyme and cook until the mushrooms are soft.	2	Add the wine then bring to a boil and cook until the liquid has reduced by half.
3	Toast the bread until golden on both sides. Brush with olive oil and rub with garlic halves.	4	Serve the bread topped with the mushrooms and finished with the cheese and chives.

MUSHROOM YAKITORI

❧ SERVES: 2 TO 4 AS A STARTER • PREPARATION: 15 MINUTES • COOKING: 10 MINUTES ❧

3 tablespoons (45 ml) soy sauce
1 tablespoon (15 ml) mirin
1 tablespoon (15 ml) sake
2 teaspoons (10 ml) superfine granulated
  sugar

1 pound (500 g) button mushrooms
6 green onions, cut into 2-inch (5 cm)
  pieces
Sea salt flakes, to taste

NOTE:
If using bamboo skewers, soak them in a
bowl of water before using to prevent them
burning while cooking.

1 2
3 4

1	Put the soy, mirin, sake and sugar in a saucepan and stir over low heat until the sugar dissolves, then boil until slightly thickened.	2	Thread the mushrooms and spring onions onto several pre-soaked wooden skewers. Sprinkle the salt over.
3	Cook on a preheated grill, grill pan or barbecue until tender, brushing a couple of times during cooking with the sauce.	4	Dip the skewers in the sauce before serving.

ONIONS

6

FRENCH ONION SOUP

❧ SERVES: 4 TO 6 • PREPARATION: 20 MINUTES • COOKING: 40 MINUTES ❧

2 pounds (1 kg) onions
3 tablespoons (45 ml) butter
3 tablespoons (45 ml) olive oil

4 cups (1 L) beef stock
½ cup (125 ml) white wine
1 bay leaf

1 small loaf French bread
½ cup (70 g) grated Gruyère or
   Emmentaler cheese

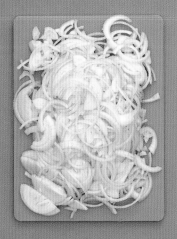

1 2
3 4

1	Slice the onions.	2	Fry the onions in the butter and oil until caramelized. Add the stock, wine and bay leaf. Boil for 5 minutes, then simmer for 20 minutes.
3	Slice the bread and toast one side until golden brown. Sprinkle grated cheese over and grill until the cheese melts.	4	Put the bread into serving bowls and ladle the soup over. Serve extra grated cheese on the side for your guests.

ONION FLAN

❧ SERVES: 4 TO 6 • PREPARATION: 20 MINUTES • COOKING: 45 MINUTES ❧

3 tablespoons (45 ml) olive oil
1½ pounds (750 g) onions, sliced
2 tomatoes, chopped

1 sheet puff pastry
12 anchovy fillets, halved
12 small black olives, pitted and halved

NOTE:
This traditional French dish is called pissal-dière in France.

1	Preheat oven to 400°F (200°C). Heat the oil in a saucepan, add the onions, cover and cook for 15 minutes, until caramelized.	2	Add the tomatoes and cook for 10 minutes, or until all the liquid has been absorbed. Allow to cool slightly.
3	Spread the filling onto the pastry, leaving a ¾-inch (2 cm) border. Arrange the anchovies in a criss-cross pattern on top and top with the olives.	4	Place on a baking sheet lined with parchment paper and bake for 20 minutes, or until crisp and golden brown.

CARAMELIZED ONION TART

❧ SERVES: 8 • PREPARATION: 40 MINUTES • COOKING: 1 HOUR, 20 MINUTES ❧

PASTRY:
½ cup (125 ml) butter, chopped
2 cups (500 ml) all-purpose flour
1 egg yolk

FILLING:
6 onions (about 1 pound/500 g), sliced
2 tablespoons (30 ml) olive oil
3 eggs, lightly beaten
½ cup (125ml) heavy cream (36%)

Grated nutmeg, to taste
Sea salt and black pepper, to taste
5 ounces (150 g) goat's cheese
1 tablespoon (15 ml) chopped thyme

1 2
3 4

1	Preheat oven to 400°F (200°C). Rub the butter into the flour until it resembles fine bread crumbs.	2	Cut in the egg yolk and 2 tablespoons (30 ml) ice water and mix until the dough comes together. Gather the dough into a ball.
3	Roll the dough out to fit a 9-inch (23 cm) loose-bottomed tart pan. Chill for 20 minutes. Fry the onions in the oil until caramelized.	4	Roll a rolling pin over the top of the tin to remove any leftover pastry. ➢

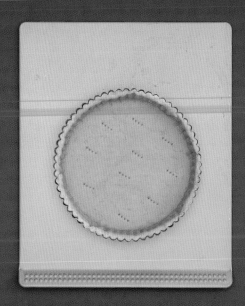

5 6
7 8

5	Line the tart crust with parchment paper and cover with rice or baking beans and bake for 15 minutes, or until golden.	6	Remove the rice or beans and paper, prick the pastry base with a fork and bake until the pastry is dry. Set aside.
7	Whisk the eggs, cream and nutmeg together in a bowl. Season with salt and pepper.	8	Sprinkle the onions over the base of the baked pastry, pour the egg mixture over and scatter the goat's cheese and thyme on top.

 9 Reduce the oven temperature to 350°F (180°C) and bake the tart for 20 minutes, or until the filling is golden and set.

VARIATION
❋

This tart is equally tasty made with blue cheese — use the same quantity as the goat's cheese — Roquefort or Stilton works well.

BAKED SHALLOTS

❧ SERVES: 4 TO 6 • PREPARATION: 10 MINUTES • COOKING: 40 MINUTES ❧

6 shallots
¾ cup (175 ml) heavy cream (36%)
1 ounce (30 g) spicy salami, chopped

½ ounce (15 g) Parmesan cheese, grated
   (about 2½ tablespoons/37 ml)

1 2
3 4

1	Preheat oven to 350°F (180°C). Bring the shallots to a boil in a pot of salted water. Reduce the heat and simmer until just tender.	2	Slice the shallots in half and put in a 1-quart (1 L) ovenproof dish.
3	Pour the cream over, then sprinkle over the salami and cheese.	4	Bake for 30 minutes, or until golden brown and bubbling.

LEEK & POTATO SOUP

➥ SERVES: 6 • PREPARATION: 20 MINUTES • COOKING: 40 MINUTES ⭅

¼ cup (60 ml) butter
4 leeks, cut into thin slices
5 medium potatoes, peeled and chopped
4 cups (1 L) chicken stock

Sea salt, to taste
½ cup (125 ml) heavy cream (36%)
1 tablespoon (15 ml) snipped chives

1 2
3 4

1	Melt the butter in a saucepan and cook the leeks over medium heat until soft.	2	Add the potatoes and cook for 5 minutes, or until soft.
3	Add the stock and bring to a boil. Reduce the heat and simmer for 30 minutes. Cool slightly then blend in a blender or food processor until smooth.	4	Season with salt. Serve the soup warm or chilled with the cream stirred through and topped with the chives.

LEEK TART

❧ SERVES: 6 • PREPARATION: 20 MINUTES • COOKING: 50 MINUTES ❧

1 tablespoon (15 ml) olive oil
2 tablespoons (30 ml) butter
2 pounds (1 kg) leeks

2 to 3 tablespoons (30 to 45 ml)
  all-purpose flour
⅔ cup (150 ml) heavy cream (36%)
Sea salt and cracked black pepper

Pinch of grated nutmeg
2 sheets puff pastry
1 egg yolk mixed with 1 teaspoon (5 ml)
water

1 2
3 4

1	Preheat oven to 400°F (200°C). Heat the oil and butter in a saucepan and cook the leeks until soft and golden.	2	Remove the pan from the heat, add the flour and mix until combined. Return to the heat and cook until golden.
3	Remove from the heat and stir in the cream, salt, pepper and nutmeg. Return to the heat and cook, stirring, until the mixture is thick. Let cool.	4	Unroll one of the pastry sheets then spread the leek mixture over it, leaving a ¾-inch (2 cm) border. Brush the border with the egg yolk mix. ➤

			NOTE
			❋

5	Cut the other pastry sheet into thin strips and arrange in a lattice pattern on the top of the filling.	Place a baking sheet in the oven when you turn it on to preheat the baking sheet. This allows the pastry to cook evenly so it becomes crisp and golden.
		This traditional dish from northern France is called flamiche in French.

6	Brush with more egg wash and bake on a baking sheet lined with parchment paper for 30 minutes, or until crisp and golden.	Try cooking some peeled and diced potatoes in with the leeks. You may also want to add some chopped parsley and chives to the mix.

LEAFY
VEGETABLES

7

Salad Leaves 56a, 56b

Salad Dressings 57a, 57b

Creamed Spinach 58

Spinach & Feta in Phyllo 59

Spinach & Ricotta Cannelloni 60

Arugula & Parmesan Salad 61

Arugula & Cilantro Pesto 62

Baked Belgian Endives 63

Chargrilled Radicchio 64

Asian Greens 65

Salsify & Mackerel Cakes 66

1 2
3 4

SALAD LEAVES

❋

1. GREEN BATAVIA: This lettuce has attractive frilly leaves, a good crunch and a nutty flavor.
2. LOLLO ROSSO: A loose-leaf lettuce with attractive frilly red leaves.
3. OAK LEAF: As the name suggests, the leaves are shaped like oak leaves.
4. LOLLO VERDE: Another loose-leaf lettuce, this time with green frilly leaves and a mild flavor.

1 2
3 4

SALAD LEAVES

❊

1. ICEBERG: This lettuce has a crisp, crunchy texture and a mild, refreshing flavor.
2. CURLY ENDIVE (FRISÉE): Part of the chicory family, this lettuce has a slightly bitter taste but is great mixed with other leaves in a salad.
3. BUTTERHEAD (ROUND): Round/butterhead – a soft-leaved lettuce with a mild flavor.
4. FED BUTTERHEAD (RED ROUND): Has pretty red-tinged leaves and a mild, sweet flavor, which makes a good contrast when teamed with other leaves.

1 2 3 4 5 6

SALAD LEAVES

✻

1. **RADICCHIO:** Italian for chicory, this lettuce has a bitter flavor.
2. **LITTLE GEM:** A variety of Romaine but smaller and more compact, with crumpled leaves and a good flavor.
3. **RED ENDIVE AND 4. BELGIAN ENDIVE:** Has a distinct peppery flavor so should be used sparingly in salads.
5. **DANDELION GREENS:** Leaves are best eaten when young and tender; they have a bitter flavor.
6. **ROMAINE:** Also called romaine lettuce, this variety has a tightly packed head of crisp leaves and a delicious flavor.

SALAD LEAVES

— ❃ —

Use a mixture of leafy greens, such as the ones here, and then choose a dressing (see recipes 57a and 57b) to complement the salad and the rest of the meal.

1. MÂCHE (LAMB'S LETTUCE)   **3. ARUGULA**   **5. BABY SPINACH**   **7. MUSTARD GREENS**

2. RED CHARD   **4. WATERCRESS SPROUTS**   **6. WATERCRESS**

SALAD DRESSINGS

❧ PREPARATION: 10 MINUTES • COOKING: NONE ❧

ITALIAN DRESSING (MAKES 2 OUNCES/60 ML)
Whisk together 1 tablespoon (15 ml) each of white vinegar, chopped fresh basil, ½ teaspoon (2 ml) superfine granulated sugar and 3 tablespoons (45 ml) extra virgin olive oil.

BALSAMIC DRESSING (MAKES 3 OUNCES/90 ML)
Whisk together 2 tablespoons (30 ml) balsamic vinegar, 1 tablespoon (15 ml) Dijon mustard, 1 minced garlic clove and 3 tablespoons (45 ml) olive oil.

SALAD DRESSINGS

❖ PREPARATION: 10 MINUTES • COOKING: NONE ❖

THAI DRESSING (MAKES 5 OUNCES/150 ML)
Whisk together 2 tablespoons (30 ml) each of fish sauce, lime juice and brown sugar with ½ teaspoon (2 ml) sesame oil, 1 tablespoon (15 ml) chopped cilantro and 4 tablespoons (60 ml) peanut oil.

BLUE CHEESE (MAKES 5¼ OUNCES/160 ML)
Blend together 2½ ounces (75 g) Roquefort cheese with 3 tablespoons (45 ml) each light cream or half-and-half and olive oil and 1 tablespoon (15 ml) each white wine vinegar and water.

SALAD DRESSINGS

❖ PREPARATION: 10 MINUTES • COOKING: NONE ❖

TAHINI CREAM (MAKES 4 OUNCES/120 ML)
Whisk together 2 tablespoons (30 ml) each of tahini paste and orange juice with 1 tablespoon (15 ml) red wine vinegar and 3 tablespoons (45 ml) water to form a creamy dressing.

VINAIGRETTE (MAKES 2 OUNCES/60 ML)
Whisk together 1 tablespoon (15 ml) white wine vinegar, a generous pinch of salt and 3 tablespoons (45 ml) extra virgin olive oil.

SALAD DRESSINGS

⇥ PREPARATION: 10 MINUTES • COOKING: NONE ⇤

HORSERADISH, CHIVE & YOGURT (MAKES 2¾ OUNCES/80 ML)
Whisk 2 teaspoons (10 ml) horseradish, 1 teaspoon (5 ml) each of honey and chopped chives and 3 tablespoons (45 ml) Greek yogurt; thin with water.

ORANGE, GARLIC & MUSTARD (MAKES 3 OUNCES/90 ML)
Whisk 1 tablespoon (15 ml) each of white wine vinegar and whole-grain mustard, 1 minced garlic and 2 tablespoons (30 ml) each of orange juice and extra virgin olive oil.

CREAMED SPINACH

❧ SERVES: 4 • PREPARATION: 5 MINUTES • COOKING: 10 MINUTES ❧

1 pound (500 g) spinach, washed and
  trimmed
3 tablespoons (45 ml) butter
3 green onions, thinly sliced

½ cup (125 ml) heavy cream (36%)
Grated nutmeg, to taste
Sea salt and cracked black pepper, to taste

1 2
3 4

1	Put the spinach in a large bowl and cover with boiling water. Let stand until the spinach wilts.	2	Allow the spinach to cool slightly, then finely chop to shred.
3	Heat the butter in a frying pan and cook the green onions for 3 minutes, or until soft.	4	Add the spinach, cream, nutmeg, salt and pepper. Bring to a boil, reduce the heat and simmer for 3 minutes; serve.

SPINACH & FETA IN PHYLLO

❖ MAKES: 16 • PREPARATION: 30 MINUTES • COOKING: 30 MINUTES ❖

2¼ pounds (1kg) spinach or Swiss chard
  leaves, washed and trimmed
1 tablespoon (15 ml) olive oil
8 green onions, sliced
2 tablespoons (30 ml) chopped mint

2 tablespoons (30 ml) chopped dill
1 teaspoon (5 ml) sugar
1 teaspooon (5 ml) black pepper
⅔ cup (150 ml) ricotta cheese
8 ounces (250 g) feta cheese, crumbled
  (about 2 cups/500 ml)

½ cup (125 ml) grated mozzarella
2 eggs, lightly beaten
2 tablespoons (30 ml) olive oil
⅓ cup (75 ml) butter, melted
1 pound (500 g) filo pastry

1 2
3 4

1	Preheat oven to 400°F (200°C). Put the spinach in a bowl and pour boiling water over and let wilt.	2	Once cool, drain and squeeze out any excess moisture. Finely chop to shred the spinach.	
3	Heat the oil in a frying pan and cook the green onions for 2 minutes, then transfer to a bowl.	4	Add the mint, dill, sugar, pepper, cheeses and eggs and mix well to combine.	➤

5 6
7 8

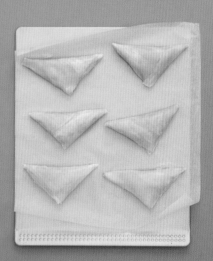

5	Combine the oil and melted butter. Put one sheet of phyllo on a work surface and brush with the oil mixture; continue layering and brushing until you have used 4 of the sheets.	6	Cut the sheets in 2 or 4 even strips (depending on the size of the sheets of phyllo) and put 1 tablespoon (15 ml) of the filling onto one end.
7	Roll up the pastry by working from one end to the other to form a triangle.	8	Place the triangles on a baking sheet lined with parchment paper.

	Bake for 15 to 20 minutes, or until crisp and golden brown.	**NOTES** ※
9		You can cut the phyllo into smaller strips (to make smaller triangles) and serve the pastries as finger food at parties. The uncooked pastries can be frozen and baked without being thawed.

SPINACH & RICOTTA CANNELLONI

❧ SERVES: 4 • PREPARATION: 40 MINUTES • COOKING: 40 MINUTES ❧

2¼ pounds (1 kg) spinach, washed, trimmed, wilted, then cooled and shredded
3 green onions, chopped
2 garlic cloves, finely chopped
1¼ cups (310 ml) ricotta cheese

Grated nutmeg, to taste
Sea salt and black pepper, to taste
12 ounces (375 g) fresh lasagna sheets
3 cups (750 ml) tomato passata or tomato
sauce

2 tablespoons (30 ml) torn basil leaves
½ cup (125 ml) grated Parmesan cheese

1 2
3 4

1	Preheat oven to 400°F (200°C). Put the shredded spinach, green onions, garlic, ricotta, nutmeg, salt and pepper in a bowl.	2	Cut the lasagna sheets in half and put 2 tablespoons (30 ml) of the filling onto one end of each half-sheet.	
3	Roll the lasagna sheets up to enclose the filling.	4	Fit the rolls into a 2-quart (2 L) baking dish.	➤

		NOTE
5	Pour the passata or sauce over the cannelloni and sprinkle the top with basil and Parmesan. Cover with foil and bake for 20 minutes.	Allow the cannelloni to stand for 15 minutes before serving, as this makes cutting and serving easier, so the cannelloni won't fall apart.

6 | Uncover and bake for a further 20 minutes, or until the cheese is golden. Serve.

You can use dried cannelloni tubes or large dried pasta shells for this dish, but you will need to add ½ cup (125 ml) water to the sauce and increase the cooking time in accordance with the package instructions.

ARUGULA & PARMESAN SALAD

⇌ SERVES: 4 • PREPARATION: 5 MINUTES • COOKING: NONE ⇌

8 ounces (250 g) arugula
3½ ounces (100 g) Parmesan cheese
1 tablespoon (15 ml) balsamic vinegar
2 tablespoons (30 ml) olive oil

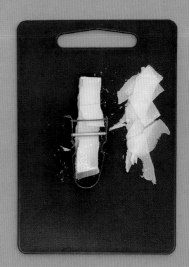

1 2
3 4

1	Wash the arugula leaves and pat dry with paper towels.	2	Use a sharp vegetable peeler to shave the Parmesan cheese.
3	Whisk the vinegar and olive oil together in a small bowl.	4	Arrange the arugula and Parmesan shavings on a serving plate and drizzle the dressing over.

ARUGULA & CILANTRO PESTO

❧ SERVES: 4 • PREPARATION: 10 MINUTES • COOKING: 5 MINUTES ❧

2 tablespoons (30 ml) pine nuts
2 cups (500 ml) arugula leaves
1 cup (250 ml) cilantro leaves
2 garlic cloves
2 tablespoons (30 ml) pumpkin seeds

½ cup (125 ml) grated pecorino cheese
Sea salt, to taste
3 tablespoons (45 ml) olive oil
Your choice of pasta, to serve

1 2
3 4

1	Toast the pine nuts in a dry frying pan for about 5 minutes, or until they start to turn golden. Keep a close eye on them.	2	Put the arugula, cilantro, garlic, pine nuts, pumpkin seeds, cheese and salt into a food processor or blender and process until smooth.
3	Gradually add the oil and mix well to combine.	4	Serve the pesto tossed through pasta, or as a topping for baked vegetables.

BAKED BELGIAN ENDIVES

➤ SERVES: 4 • PREPARATION: 10 MINUTES • COOKING: 40 MINUTES ➤

4 Belgian endives, trimmed
1 tablespoon (15 ml) olive oil
1 small onion, sliced

1 cup (250 ml) chicken stock
Sea salt and black pepper, to taste
⅓ cup (75 ml) fresh bread crumbs
¼ cup (60 ml) grated Parmesan cheese

1 garlic clove, crushed
1 tablespoon (15 ml) chopped parsley
1 tablespoon (15 ml) chopped oregano

1 2
3 4

1	Preheat oven to 350°F (180°C). Cut the endives in half. Heat the oil in a frying pan and brown the onion over medium heat. Add the endives and brown.	2	Transfer the endive mixture to a 1-quart (1 L) baking dish and pour the stock over. Season with salt and pepper.
3	Combine the bread crumbs, Parmesan, garlic and herbs and sprinkle over the endive mixture.	4	Bake for 30 minutes, or until the endives are soft and the crumbs are golden brown.

CHARGRILLED RADICCHIO

❖ SERVES: 4 • PREPARATION: 5 MINUTES • COOKING: 10 MINUTES ❖

3 radicchio
2 tablespoons (30 ml) olive oil
2 garlic cloves, finely chopped

1 tablespoon (15 ml) balsamic vinegar
1 teaspoon (5 ml) superfine granulated
  sugar
Sea salt and black pepper, to taste

1 2
3 4

1	Cut the radicchio into quarters.	2	Whisk the oil, garlic, vinegar, sugar and salt and pepper together in a small bowl.
3	Put some of the radicchio in a large bowl, then add a little of the dressing and toss generously until coated. Repeat with the remaining leaves and dressing.	4	Cook the radicchio on a grill pan, indoor grill or barbecue until wilted, then serve.

ASIAN GREENS

❖ SERVES: 4 • PREPARATION: 5 MINUTES • COOKING: 5 MINUTES ❖

1 bunch Chinese broccoli (gai-lan) or Asian
  greens of your choice, such as bok choy or
  napa cabbage (Chinese cabbage)
1 teaspoon (5 ml) roasted sesame oil
2 tablespoons (30 ml) oyster sauce

1 2
3 4

1	Cut the greens in half and arrange on a plate.	2	Put the plate in a bamboo steamer.
3	Set the bamboo steamer over gently simmering water in a wok. Cover and cook for 5 minutes, until greens brighten and become tender.	4	Drizzle over sesame oil and oyster sauce and serve.

SALSIFY & MACKEREL CAKES

❧ SERVES: 4 • PREPARATION: 15 MINUTES • COOKING: 30 MINUTES ❧

1 pound (500 g) salsify
1 tablespoon (15 ml) lemon juice
3½ ounces (100 g) smoked mackerel, flaked
Sea salt and black pepper, to taste
All-purpose flour, to dust

2 tablespoons (30 ml) butter
1 tablespoon (15 ml) olive oil
4 to 6 gherkins, chopped
1 hard-boiled egg, chopped
1 tablespoon (15 ml) capers

1 2
3 4

1	Scrub the salsify to clean then peel and chop, putting it in water with the lemon to prevent discoloration. Boil the salsify in the water and lemon juice until soft.	2	Drain the salsify, put into a bowl and mash.	
3	Add the mackerel, season with salt and pepper and, using ¼ cup (60 ml) of the mix at a time, shape into patties, then coat in the flour.	4	Heat the butter and oil in a frying pan and cook the patties until golden, flipping once to brown both sides.	➤

		VARIATION
	Mix the gherkins, chopped egg and capers together in a bowl.	You can use smoked chicken instead of the smoked mackerel, if you prefer.
5		

| 6 | Serve the warm patties with the gherkin and egg mixture. | **TIP**
❋
It is important that you put the salsify in the water and lemon as soon as you peel it, as it discolors rapidly. |

PODS & SEEDS

8

French-style Peas 67
Pasta Primavera 68
Pea & Ham Soup 69
Broad Bean Bruschetta 70
Broad Beans with Chorizo 71
Beans with Samphire Butter 72
Stir-fried Snow Peas 73
Braised Greek-style Beans 74
Broccoli with Raisins 75
Corn & Chicken Soup 76
Corn Fritters 77

FRENCH-STYLE PEAS

❧ SERVES: 4 • PREPARATION: 10 MINUTES • COOKING: 30 MINUTES ❧

2 flat-leaf parsley sprigs
2 thyme sprigs
2 rosemary sprigs
1½ pounds (750 g) fresh or frozen peas,
   (about 1½ cups/375 ml)

1 green onion, chopped
1 small head of Romaine lettuce, finely
   shredded
½ cup (125 ml) white wine
2½ (40 ml) tablespoons butter

1 teaspoon (5 ml) superfine granulated
   sugar
Sea salt and cracked black pepper, to taste

1 2
3 4

1	Tie the herbs together with kitchen string.	2	Put the peas, green onion, lettuce, wine and the bunch of tied herbs in a saucepan and bring to a boil.
3	Cover and simmer for 30 minutes, or until the peas have changed color.	4	Remove the herbs and stir in the butter, sugar and season with salt and pepper.

PASTA PRIMAVERA

❧ SERVES: 4 • PREPARATION: 15 MINUTES • COOKING: 20 MINUTES ❧

5 ounces (150 g) broad beans
12 ounces (340 g) fresh tagliatelle
5 ounces (150 g) asparagus, cut into
bite-sized pieces
3½ ounces (100 g) sugar snap peas
4 ounces (120 g) fresh or frozen peas, about

1 cup/250 ml)
2 garlic cloves, finely chopped
1 fennel bulb, sliced
1 tablespoon (15 ml) olive oil
2 tablespoons (30 ml) butter
½ cup (125 ml) white wine

1 cup (250 ml) heavy cream (36%)
1 tablespoon (15 ml) chopped parsley
1 tablespoon (15 ml) chopped oregano
3½ ounces (100 g) cherry tomatoes
1¾ ounces (50 g) Parmesan cheese
Sea salt and black pepper, to taste

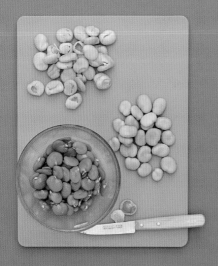

1 2
3 4

1	Boil the broad beans until tender. Rinse under cold running water, then drain and shell. Cook the pasta; drain.	2	Boil the asparagus, sugar snap peas and peas until tender. Rinse under cold water to set color and drain.
3	Fry garlic and fennel in the oil and butter. Add wine and boil until reduced by half. Add cream, herbs and tomatoes and cook for 5 minutes.	4	Add the vegetables, pasta and Parmesan to the sauce. Season with salt and pepper and cook until heated through.

PEA & HAM SOUP

❖ SERVES: 6 • PREPARATION: 20 MINUTES • COOKING: 1 HOUR ❖

1 tablespoon (15 ml) olive oil
1½ tablespoons (22 ml) butter
1 carrot, chopped
2 celery sticks, chopped

1 onion, chopped
1 ham bone (about 2 pounds/1 kg))
1 cinnamon stick
3 cloves

1½ cups (125 ml) split green peas
2 cups (500 ml) fresh or frozen peas
Sea salt and black pepper, to taste

1 2
3 4

1	Heat the oil and butter in a pot and cook the carrot, celery and onion until soft. Add the ham, 6 cups (1.5 L) water and the spices.	2	Bring to a boil and cook for 1 hour, or until the ham falls off the bone, skimming the surface during cooking to remove any impurities.	
3	Remove the ham bone and allow to cool slightly before removing the meat from it.	4	Remove the cinnamon stick from the soup. Add the split peas and fresh peas and boil for 10 minutes, or until soft.	➤

| 7 | Puree the soup in a blender or food processor until smooth and return to the pot. | **VARIATION**
❋
This soup makes a delicious filling for small tart cases, which are fabulous to serve as finger food — serve hot or cold, you can finish them with a drizzle of extra virgin olive oil and cracked black pepper, if desired. |

8	Add the ham back to the soup and season with salt and pepper before serving.	**NOTE:** ❊
		If you prefer a chunkier soup, do not puree it, just use a potato masher to crush the peas.

BROAD BEAN BRUSCHETTA

❖ SERVES: 4 • PREPARATION: 10 MINUTES • COOKING: 20 MINUTES ❖

10 ounces (300 g) broad beans (horse beans, fava beans)
½ cup (125 ml) fresh or frozen peas
1 tablespoon (15 ml) olive oil, plus extra for brushing

2 garlic cloves, 1 chopped and 1 halved
1 onion, chopped
2 tablespoons (30 ml) butter
3 tablespoons (45 ml) grated Parmesan cheese

2 tablespoons (30 ml) finely shredded mint
8 slices ciabatta
Cracked black pepper, to taste

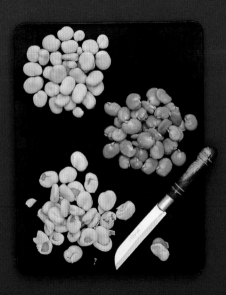

1 2
3 4

1	Boil the broad beans until tender. Rinse then drain and shell. Boil the peas until tender, then rinse and drain.	2	Heat the oil in a frying pan and cook the chopped garlic and onion for 5 minutes, or until the onion is golden brown.
3	Combine the onion, chopped garlic, beans and peas in a bowl, add the butter and Parmesan and roughly mash. Stir the mint through.	4	Toast the bread until golden, brush with oil and rub with the halved garlic. Top with the bean mixture and season with pepper.

BROAD BEANS WITH CHORIZO

❖ SERVES: 4 • PREPARATION: 25 MINUTES • COOKING: 30 MINUTES ❖

1 pound (500 g) broad beans (horse beans, fava beans)
1 chorizo
1 tablespoon (15 ml) olive oil
2 garlic cloves

2 dried red chilies
½ cup (125 ml) white wine
½ cup (125 ml) chicken stock
1 rosemary sprig

1 2
3 4

1	Boil the broad beans and chorizo together in a pan until tender. Drain and shell the broad beans.	2	Slice the chorizo. Heat the oil in a deep frying pan and cook the chorizo for 5 minutes, or until browned.
3	Add the garlic, chilies, wine, stock and rosemary. Bring to a boil and cook for 5 minutes, until reduced by half. Reduce to a simmer.	4	Return the beans to the pan and cook until heated through, then serve.

BEANS WITH SAMPHIRE BUTTER

❖ SERVES: 4 • PREPARATION: 25 MINUTES • COOKING: 20 MINUTES ❖

7 ounces (200 g) samphire
1 pound (500 g) green beans
3 tablespoons (45 ml) butter, softened
1 garlic clove, crushed
2 teaspoons (10 ml) lemon juice
Sea salt and black pepper, to taste

NOTE:
"Samphire" refers to two very similar edible plants. Rock samphire (Crithmum maritimum) is found in coastal areas across Great Britain and northwestern Europe.

Also called salicornia, glasswort and sea bean, North American samphire is of the genus Salicornia and grows along the Pacific and Atlantic coasts. Both types of samphire are spindly, spiky plants with a distinct maritime flavor.

1 2
3 4

1	Wash the samphire and pick over, discarding any withered pieces.	2	Boil the samphire until tender. Drain well.
3	Trim the beans and boil until bright green and tender. Drain well.	4	Melt the butter, add the garlic and cook until golden. Add the beans and samphire and toss in the lemon juice. Season and serve.

STIR-FRIED SNOW PEAS

❧ SERVES: 4 • PREPARATION: 15 MINUTES • COOKING: 15 MINUTES ❧

½ teaspoon (2 ml) sesame oil
1 tablespoon (15 ml) peanut oil
1 onion, thinly sliced
2 garlic cloves, sliced

10 ounces (300 g) snow peas
7 ounces (200 g) baby sugar snap peas
3½ ounces (100 g) baby sweetcorn
1 tablespoon (15 ml) kecap manis

1 tablespoon (15 ml) soy sauce
1 teaspoon (5 ml) superfine granulated
   sugar

1 2
3 4

1	Heat the sesame and peanut oils in a wok and stir-fry the onion and garlic for 5 minutes, or until golden.	2	Add the snow peas, sugar snap peas, baby corn and 1 tablespoon (15 ml) water and stir-fry until bright green.
3	Mix the kecap manis, soy sauce and sugar together, then add to the wok and stir-fry until the sauce is heated through.	4	Serve immediately with rice or noodles.

BRAISED GREEK-STYLE BEANS

❖ SERVES: 6 • PREPARATION: 15 MINUTES • COOKING: 3 HOURS ❖

1½ pounds (750 g) green beans
1 large onion, sliced
1½ cups (375 ml) olive oil
1 bay leaf

3 garlic cloves, finely sliced
1 teaspoon (5 ml) superfine granulated sugar
1 teaspoon (5 ml) salt
1 cup (250 ml) tomato passata or tomato
   sauce

1 2
3 4

1	Preheat oven to 300°F (150°C). Wash and trim the beans.	2	Bring the beans, onion, oil, bay leaf, garlic, sugar, salt, passata or sauce and 1 cup (250 ml) water to a boil in a large ovenproof pot.
3	Cover the top with wet parchment paper and a tight-fitting lid.	4	Bake for 3 hours. The beans are best served at room temperature.

BROCCOLI WITH RAISINS

✦ SERVES: 4 • PREPARATION: 15 MINUTES • COOKING: 15 MINUTES ✦

1 pound (500 g) broccoli, cut into florets
⅓ cup (75 ml) butter
1 teaspoon (5 ml) orange zest

⅓ cup (75 ml) raisins
2 tablespoons (30 ml) pine nuts, toasted
Sea salt and black pepper, to taste

1 2
3 4

1	Steam the broccoli in a bamboo steamer over a pot of gently simmering water until tender.	2	Stop the broccoli from cooking by plunging it into a bowl of ice water.
3	Melt the butter in a frying pan with the orange zest, add the raisins and pine nuts and cook for 3 minutes.	4	Toss through the broccoli, then season with salt and pepper and serve.

CORN & CHICKEN SOUP

❖ SERVES: 4 • PREPARATION: 10 MINUTES • COOKING: 40 MINUTES ❖

2 corn cobs
6 cups (1.5 L) chicken stock
⅓ cup (75 ml) Shaoxing wine (Chinese rice wine)

5 slices fresh ginger
3 garlic cloves, thinly sliced
6 green onions, sliced

2 chicken breasts, sliced
2 eggs, lightly beaten
1 teaspoon (5 ml) soy sauce
½ teaspoon (2 ml) white pepper

1 2
3 4

1	Cut the corn kernels from the cobs.	2	Bring the stock and wine to a boil. Add the corn, ginger, garlic, half the green onions and the chicken. Simmer for 30 minutes.
3	Add the beaten eggs in a slow, steady stream so that it forms threads in the soup. Season with the soy sauce and white pepper.	4	Serve the soup topped with the remaining green onions.

CORN FRITTERS

❧ SERVES: 4 (MAKES 16) • PREPARATION: 30 MINUTES • COOKING: 40 MINUTES ❧

1 cup (125 g) all-purpose flour
1 teaspoon (5 ml) baking powder
½ teaspoon (2 ml) baking soda
Sea salt and white pepper, to taste
1 tablespoon (15 ml) superfine granulated sugar

2 eggs, lightly beaten
¾ cup (175 ml) buttermilk
3 corn cobs, kernels removed (about 2 cups/500 ml)
3 green onions, sliced

3 tablespoons (45 ml) chopped cilantro
1 tablespoon (15 ml) chopped chives
3 tablespoons (45 ml) olive oil
5 ounces (150 g) smoked salmon
Lemon wedges, to serve

1 2
3 4

| 1 | Sift the flour, baking powder and baking soda into a bowl. Stir in the salt, pepper and sugar. | 2 | Whisk the eggs and buttermilk together in a bowl and add to the dry ingredients. Mix until smooth. |
| 3 | Stir the corn kernels, green onions and herbs into the batter. | 4 | Heat the oil in a large non-stick frying pan and add 2 tablespoons (30 ml) of the batter for each fritter. ➢ |

| 5 | Cook the fritters in batches. Flip so both sides are golden brown and the fritters are cooked through. | **NOTE**
❋
Since the fritters are cooked in batches, keep them warm in a low oven while you finish cooking the rest. |

6

Serve the fritters with smoked salmon and
lemon wedges.

VARIATION
❋

These fritters are also great served with some baby
spinach and sour cream on the side.

DESSERTS & BEVERAGES

9

Sweet Carrot Soup 78
Pumpkin Pie 79
Carrot Cake 80
Beet Brownies 81
Chocolate Zucchini Cake 82
Smoothies 83
Juices 84

SWEET CARROT SOUP

✦ SERVES: 4 • PREPARATION: 15 MINUTES • COOKING: 40 MINUTES ✦

10 ounces (300 g) carrots, peeled and
  chopped
⅔ cup (150 ml) milk
¼ teaspoon (1 ml) ground coriander

½ teaspoon (2 ml) ground cinnamon
Pinch of grated nutmeg
⅔ cup (150 ml) coconut milk
⅔ cup (150 ml) sweetened condensed milk

1 teaspoon (5 ml) vanilla extract
Toasted shredded coconut, to serve

1 2
3 4

1	Put the carrots in a saucepan and add the milk, ⅔ cup (150 ml) water and spices.	2	Simmer over a low heat for 30 minutes, or until very soft.
3	Transfer to a bowl, add the coconut milk, condensed milk and vanilla. Transfer to a food processor and process until smooth.	4	Chill for 1 hour before serving. Serve sprinkled with shredded coconut.

PUMPKIN PIE

SERVES: 8 • PREPARATION: 40 MINUTES • COOKING: 1 HOUR

PASTRY:
2 cups (500 ml) all-purpose flour
½ cup (125 ml) butter, chopped
¼ cup (60 ml) superfine granulated sugar
2 egg yolks
1 teaspoon (5 ml) vanilla extract

FILLING:
1 pound (500 g) pumpkin, peeled and
  chopped
2 eggs, lightly beaten
1 cup (250 ml) brown sugar
1 teaspoon (5 ml) each ground cinnamon
  and nutmeg
½ teaspoon (2 ml) each ground ginger and salt
1 cup (250 ml) milk
¼ cup (60 ml) butter, melted
1 tablespoon (15 ml) cornstarch
Confectioner's sugar, to dust

1 2
3 4

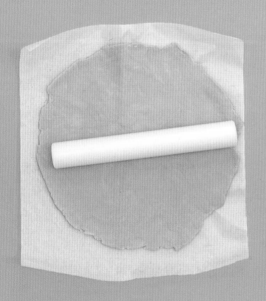

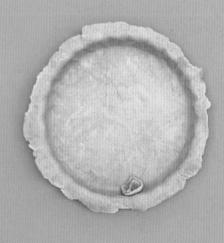

1	Preheat oven to 400°F (200°C). Rub the flour and butter together. Cut in the sugar, egg yolks, vanilla and enough iced water to form a dough.	2	Put the pumpkin in a large roasting pan and bake until very soft.	
3	Turn the dough out onto a floured board and form into a ball. Roll out the pastry between 2 sheets of parchment paper.	4	Fit the pastry into a 9-inch (23 cm) pie plate.	➢

5 6
7 8

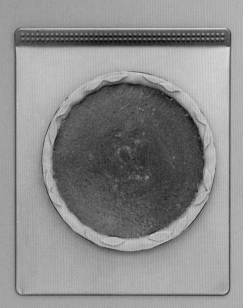

5	Trim the edges to remove any overhanging pastry.	6	Pass the pumpkin through a sieve, into a bowl. Increase the oven temperature to 450°F (230°C) and put a baking sheet in to heat.
7	Whisk the pumpkin, eggs, sugar, spices, milk and butter in a bowl.	8	Pour the pumpkin mixture into the unbaked pastry shell and bake for 10 minutes.

| 9 | Reduce the oven temperature to 350°F (180°C) and cook for a further 20 minutes, or until set. Allow to cool, dust with confectioner's sugar and serve with ice cream, if desired. | **VARIATION**
※
For a nice, crisp pastry, allow the filling to cool completely before putting it in the pastry shell. |

CARROT CAKE

❧ SERVES: 8 • PREPARATION: 20 MINUTES • COOKING: 40 MINUTES ❧

1 cup (250 ml) olive oil, plus extra
   for oiling
4 eggs, lightly beaten
1 cup (250 ml) brown sugar
1 teaspoon (5 ml) grated orange zest
2 cups (500 ml) all-purpose flour

2 teaspoons (10 ml) baking powder
1 teaspoon (5 ml) baking soda
2 teaspoons (10 ml) ground cinnamon
½ teaspoon (2 ml) ground ginger
½ teaspoon (2 ml) grated nutmeg
14 ounces (400 g) carrots, grated

⅓ cup (75 ml) walnuts, roughly chopped
1 cup (250 ml) cream cheese, softened
1½ cups (375 ml) confectioner's sugar
2 tablespoons (30 ml) milk

1 2
3 4

1	Preheat oven to 350°F (180°C). Oil a 9-inch (23 cm) springform pan. Whisk the eggs, sugar orange zest and oil until combined.	2	Sift the flour, baking powder, baking soda and spices together.	
3	Fold the dry ingredients into the egg mixture. Add the carrots and walnuts and gently mix to combine.	4	Spoon the mixture into the prepared pan. Bake for 40 minutes, until the cake comes away from the side of the tin.	➤

		VARIATION
		✳
5	Cool the cake in the pan for 10 minutes before transferring to a wire rack to cool. Meanwhile, beat the cream cheese, confectioner's sugar and milk together in a bowl until smooth.	You can cook the cake in 2 springform cake pans and then sandwich the layers together with cream or make a double batch of the cream cheese icing, if desired.

| 6 | Once the cake is completely cooled, spread the icing over the top of the cake, swirling with the back of a spoon, and serve. | **NOTE**
❋
This cake keeps for about 5 days if stored in an airtight container; if it lasts that long! |

BEET BROWNIES

❧ MAKES: 24 • PREPARATION: 20 MINUTES • COOKING: 40 MINUTES ❧

⅔ cup (150 ml) butter, plus extra for
  greasing
5 ounces (150 g) dark chocolate, chopped
3 eggs, lightly beaten
1½ cups (375 ml) dark brown sugar

1 teaspoon (5 ml) vanilla extract
1 cup (250 ml) all-purpose flour, sifted
½ teaspoon (2 ml) baking soda
¼ cup (60 ml) cocoa powder

1 cup (250 ml) grated beets
¾ cup (175 ml) raspberries

1 2
3 4

1	Preheat oven to 350°F (180°C) and grease and line an 8x8-inch (20x20 cm) square cake pan. In a heat-proof bowl over a pan of simmering water, melt the butter and chocolate.	2	Remove from the heat. Whisk the eggs, sugar and vanilla extract together in a bowl.
3	Add the melted chocolate and the sifted flour, baking soda and cocoa. Fold in the beets and raspberries and pour into the prepared pan.	4	Bake for 40 minutes, or until the brownies are slightly risen but still moist in the center. Cool and cut into squares. Dust with confectioner's sugar.

CHOCOLATE ZUCCHINI CAKE

➜ SERVES: 8 • PREPARATION: 20 MINUTES • COOKING: 50 MINUTES ←

⅔ cup (150 ml) butter, melted, plus extra
   for greasing
2½ cups (625 ml) all-purpose flour
½ cup (125 ml) cocoa powder, plus extra
   for dusting
2½ teaspoons (12 ml) baking powder

1½ teaspoons (7 ml) baking soda
1 teaspoon (5 ml) ground cinnamon
1 teaspoon (5 ml) ground ginger
1 teaspoon (5 ml) ground cardamom
1 cup (250 ml) dark brown sugar
2 tablespoons (30 ml) olive oil

3 eggs
1 teaspoon (5 ml) vanilla extract
1½ cups (375 ml) buttermilk
2 cups (500 ml) grated zucchini
5 ounces (150 g) dark chocolate
¼ cup (60 ml) heavy cream (36%)

1 2
3 4

1	Preheat oven to 350°F (180°C). Grease and line the base of a 9-inch (23 cm) round baking pan.	2	Sift the flour, cocoa, baking powder, baking soda and spices into a bowl and stir in the sugar. Make a well in the center.	
3	Whisk the butter, olive oil, eggs, vanilla and buttermilk together. Add the liquid to the dry ingredients and fold in the zucchini.	4	Pour the mixture into the prepared baking pan and bake for 50 minutes.	➤

		NOTE ❋
5	Melt the chocolate and cream in a heat-proof bowl set over a pan of simmering water.	The sweetness of this cake will depend on the type of cocoa and chocolate that you use and the chocolate ganache. If you want a less sweet result use chocolate with 70% or more cocoa; dark cocoa is more bitter than other types available in supermarkets.

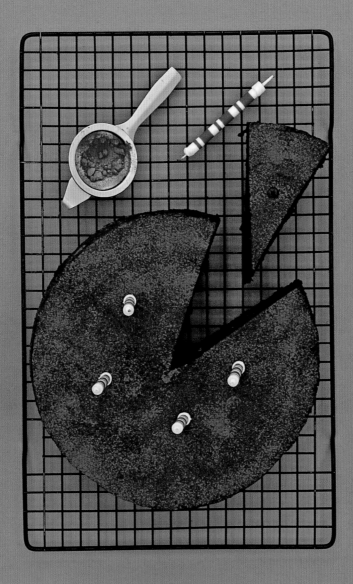

| 6 | Allow the cake to cool in the pan for 10 minutes before turning out onto a wire rack to cool completely. Spread the icing over the cooled cake and dust with cocoa. Serve with cream or ice cream, if desired. | **VARIATION**
❋
You can replace half of the zucchini with either grated carrots or grated beets, if desired. |

SMOOTHIES

❖ SERVES: 2 • PREPARATION: 5 MINUTES • COOKING: NONE ❖

GREEN SMOOTHIE: High in chlorophyll, which is an excellent source of energy.
In a blender, blend 1 cup kale, 1 chopped banana, 1 chopped pear and ½ cup (125 ml) mango nectar until smooth.

ARUGULA & STRAWBERRY: Packed with vitamin C and helps to fight off colds and boost immunity.
Blend a handful of arugula, 2 tablespoons (30 ml) cilantro, 1 chopped banana, a handful of strawberries and a handful of black seedless grapes until smooth.

SMOOTHIES

➢ SERVES: 2 • PREPARATION: 10 MINUTES • COOKING: NONE ➢

SPINACH, ORANGE & PEAR: Rich in iron; perfect for an energy boost.
In a blender, blend a handful of baby spinach leaves, 1 chopped banana, 1 chopped pear and 1 peeled and chopped orange until smooth.

AVOCADO & KIWI: Full of healthy fats; a meal in a glass.
Blend 1 chopped kiwi, 1 chopped avocado, a few sprigs of mint and ¾ cup (175 ml) chopped pineapple until smooth.

JUICES

❀ SERVES: 3 TO 4 • PREPARATION: 10 MINUTES • COOKING: NONE ❀

QUICK GAZPACHO: Full of lycopene, which may help to protect against cancer and heart disease.
Blend a little chopped cucumber, 1 garlic clove, about 20 cherry tomatoes and a few sprigs of cilantro and mint until smooth.

BEET, RASPBERRY & MINT: Great for the blood and packed with powerful antioxidants.
Blend 2 small beets that you have grated, ¾ cup (175 ml) raspberries, 1½ cups (375 ml) chopped watermelon and some grated ginger until smooth.

JUICES

❧ SERVES: 2 • PREPARATION: 5 MINUTES • COOKING: NONE ❧

CARROT & ORANGE: Packed with beta-carotene; a wonderful liver-cleansing beverage.
Blend 1 cup (250 ml) grated carrots, flesh of 1 orange, 1 banana and ½ cup (125 ml) orange-and-mango juice until smooth.

BANANA, AVOCADO & PEAR: Potassium and fiber rich, this is fantastic food for both the mind and the body.
Blend 1 chopped banana, 1 chopped avocado and 1 chopped pear until smooth.

APPENDIXES

RECIPE INDEX

GENERAL INDEX

ACKNOWLEDGMENTS

RECIPE INDEX

A
Artichokes with vinaigrette 40
Arugula & cilantro pesto 62
Arugula & Parmesan salad 61
Arugula & strawberry smoothie ... 83
Asian greens 65
Asparagus with hollandaise 39
Avocado & kiwi smoothie 83

B
Baba ghanoush 27
Baked Belgian endives 63
Baked shallots 53
Balsamic dressing 57a
Banana, avocado & pear juice 84
Beans with samphire butter 72
Beet & cheese salad 14
Beet brownies 81
Beet, raspberry & mint juice 84
Blue cheese dressing 57a
Braised Greek-style beans 74
Broad bean bruschetta 70
Broad beans with chorizo 71
Broccoli with raisins 75
Butternut squash ravioli 30
Butternut squash soup 29

C
Cabbage & pork pot stickers 35
Cabbage rolls 34
Caramelized onion tart 52
Carrot & orange juice 84
Carrot cake 80
Carrot hummus 8
Cauliflower with cheese 36
Celeriac puree 17
Chargrilled mushrooms 43
Chargrilled peppers 25
Chargrilled radicchio 64
Chocolate zucchini cake 82
Classic potato croquettes 1
Corn & chicken soup 76
Corn fritters 77
Creamed spinach 58
Creamy mushroom sauce 44

E
Eggplant parmigiana 28

F
Fennel & Parmesan salad 42
French fries 2
French onion soup 50
French-style peas 67

G
Gazpacho 22
Green smoothie 83

Guacamole 31

H
Horseradish, chive &
  yogurt dressing 57b

I
Indian vegetable curry 18
Italian dressing   57a

J
Jerusalem artichoke soup 9

L
Leek & potato soup 54
Leek tart 55

M
Minestrone soup 23
Mushroom omelet 45
Mushroom soup 47
Mushroom toasts 48
Mushroom yakitori 49

O
Onion flan 51
Orange, garlic & mustard dressing
  .... 57b
Oven-roasted vegetables 11

P
Panzanella 24
Parsnip mash 16
Pasta primavera 68
Patatas bravas 6
Pea & ham soup 69
Potatoes dauphinoise 3
Potato gnocchi 7
Potato rösti 4
Potato smash 16
Pumpkin pie 79

Q
Quick gazpacho juice 84

R
Ratatouille 21
Roast parsnips & carrots 10
Roast potatoes 5

S
Salsify & mackerel cakes 66
Seven-vegetable tagine 15
Slow-cooked fennel 41
Spinach, orange & pear
  smoothie 83
Spinach & feta in phyllo 59
Spinach & ricotta cannelloni 60
Sprouts with pancetta 37

Stir-fried broccoli & kale 38

Stir-fried snow peas 73
Stuffed peppers 33
Sweet carrot soup 78
Sweet potato chips 12
Sweet potato crumble 13
Sweet potato mash 17

T
Tahini cream 57b
Thai dressing 57a
Tomato pasta sauce 19
Tzatziki 32

V
Vegetable lasagna 20
Vinaigrette 57b

W
Wild mushroom risotto 46

Z
Zucchini fritters 26

GENERAL INDEX

A

anchovies
Onion flan................................ 51
artichokes
Artichokes with vinaigrette....... 40
Stuffed peppers 33
arugula
Beet & cheese salad.................. 14
Arugula & cilantro pesto........... 62
Arugula & Parmesan salad........ 61
Arugula & strawberry smoothie
.... 83
Asian greens 65
asparagus
Asparagus with hollandaise....... 39
Pasta primavera 68
avocados
Avocado & kiwi smoothie 83
Banana, avocado & pear
juice 84
Guacamole 31

B

Baba ghanoush 27
Balsamic dressing 57a
bananas
Arugula & strawberry smoothie
.... 83
Banana, avocado & pear
juice.................................... 84
Carrot & orange juice................ 84
Green smoothie......................... 83
Spinach, orange & pear smoothie
.... 83
beef
Cabbage rolls............................ 34
beets
Beet & cheese salad.................. 14
Beet brownies 81
Beet, raspberry & mint juice 84
Belgian endive, baked................. 63
Blue cheese dressing................. 57a
bok choy
Asian greens 65
bread
Broad bean bruschetta 70
Chargrilled peppers.................. 25
French onion soup 50
Mushroom toasts...................... 48
Panzanella 24
broad beans
Broad bean bruschetta 70
Broad beans with chorizo.......... 71
Pasta primavera 68
broccoli
Broccoli with raisins 75
Stir-fried broccoli & kale 38

Brownies, Beet............................ 81
Bruschetta, broad bean................ 70
Brussels sprouts
Sprouts with pancetta 37
butternut squash
Butternut squash ravioli 30
Butternut squash soup 29
Vegetable lasagna 20

C

cabbage
Cabbage & pork pot stickers 35
Cabbage rolls............................ 34
cakes
Beet brownies 81
Carrot cake 80
Chocolate zucchini cake........... 82
Cannelloni, spinach & ricotta 60
caperberries
Stuffed peppers 33
capers
Panzanella 24
Salsify & mackerel cakes 66
Caramelized onion tart 52
carrots
Carrot & orange juice................ 84
Carrot cake 80
Carrot hummus......................... 8
Indian vegetable curry.............. 18
Oven-roasted vegetables 11
Roast parsnips & carrots 10
Seven-vegetable tagine............. 15
Sweet carrot soup 78
cauliflower
Cauliflower with cheese 36
Indian vegetable curry.............. 18
Celeriac puree............................. 17
cheese
Eggplant parmigiana 28
Beet & cheese salad.................. 14
Blue cheese dressing................. 57a
Butternut squash ravioli 30
Caramelized onion tart 52
Cauliflower with cheese 36
Classic potato croquettes 1
Zucchini fritters....................... 26
Fennel & Parmesan salad......... 42
French onion soup 50
Mushroom toasts...................... 48
Arugula & cilantro pesto........... 62
Arugula & Parmesan salad........ 61
Slow-cooked fennel 41
Spinach & feta in phyllo 59
Spinach & ricotta cannelloni 60
Stuffed peppers 33
Vegetable lasagna 20
chestnuts

Sprouts with pancetta 37
chicken
Corn & chicken soup 76
chickpeas
Carrot hummus......................... 8
chilies
Patatas bravas.......................... 6
Chinese broccoli
Asian greens 65
Chinese cabbage
Cabbage & pork pot stickers 35
Chips, sweet potato..................... 12
chives
Horseradish, chive & yogurt
dressing 57b
chocolate
Beet brownies 81
Chocolate zucchini cake........... 82
Chorizo, broad beans with 71
cilantro
Arugula & cilantro pesto........... 62
corn
Corn fritters 77
Stir-fried snow peas.................. 73
Corn & chicken soup 76
coconut milk
Sweet carrot soup 78
couscous
Seven-vegetable tagine............. 15
Creamed spinach......................... 58
Croquettes, classic potato........... 1
Crumble, sweet potato 13
cucumber
Gazpacho 22
Tzatziki 32
Curry, Indian vegetable 18

D

daikon
Seven-vegetable tagine............. 15
dates
Beet & cheese salad.................. 14
dips
Guacamole 31
Tzatziki 32

E

eggs
Mushroom omelet..................... 45
Eggplant
Eggplant parmigiana 28
Baba ghanoush 27
Ratatouille 21
Seven-vegetable tagine 15

F

fennel
Fennel & Parmesan salad 42

Pasta primavera 68
Slow-cooked fennel 41
Vegetable lasagna 20
fettuccine
Creamy mushroom sauce 44
fish sauce
Thai dressing 57a
French fries............................... 2
French onion soup 50
French-style peas....................... 67
fritters
Corn fritters 77
Zucchini fritters...................... 26

G
garlic
Butternut squash soup 29
Orange, garlic & mustard
dressing 57b
Oven-roasted vegetables 11
Patatas bravas 6
Gazpacho.................................. 22
Quick gazpacho juice 84
Gnocchi, potato 7
goat's cheese
Beet & cheese salad................. 14
Caramelized onion tart 52
grapes
Arugula & strawberry smoothie
.... 83
green beans
Beans with samphire butter 72
Minestrone soup 23
Braised Greek-style beans.......... 74
Green smoothie.......................... 83
Guacamole 31
Pot stickers, cabbage & pork 35

H
ham
Pea & ham soup 69
Hollandaise, asparagus with 39
Horseradish, chive & yogurt
dressing 57b
Hummus, carrot 8

I
Indian vegetable curry.................. 18
Italian dressing 57a

J
Jerusalem artichoke soup 9
Juices 84

K
kale
Green smoothie.......................... 83
Stir-fried broccoli & kale 38

kiwi fruit
Avocado & kiwi smoothie 83

L
Lasagna, vegetable...................... 20
leeks
Leek tart 55

Leek & potato soup................... 54
Oven-roasted vegetables 11
lemon
Fennel & Parmesan salad 42
lettuce
French-style peas...................... 67

M
Minestrone soup........................... 23
mushrooms
Chargrilled mushrooms 43
Creamy mushroom sauce.......... 44
Mushroom omelet.................... 45
Mushroom soup 47
Mushroom toasts..................... 48
Mushroom yakitori 49
Wild mushroom risotto 46
mustard
Orange, garlic & mustard
dressing 57b

O
olives
Onion flan............................... 51
Stuffed peppers 33
Omelet, mushroom..................... 45
onions
Caramelized onion tart 52
French onion soup 50
Onion flan............................... 51
Potatoes dauphinoise 3
Ratatouille 21
oranges
Carrot & orange juice............... 84
Fennel & Parmesan salad 42
Orange, garlic & mustard
dressing 57b
Spinach, orange & pear smoothie
.... 83
Oven-roasted vegetables 11

P
Pancetta, sprouts with 37
Panzanella 24
parsnips
Roast parsnips & carrots 10
pasta
Creamy mushroom sauce.......... 44
Pasta primavera 68

Spinach & ricotta cannelloni...... 60
Tomato pasta sauce 19
pastries
Leek tart 55
Spinach & feta in phyllo 59
Patatas bravas 6
pears
Banana, avocado & pear juice ... 84
Green smoothie......................... 83
Spinach, orange & pear smoothie
.... 83
peas
Indian vegetable curry............... 18
Pasta primavera 68
Pea & ham soup 69
French-style peas....................... 67
pecans
Sweet potato crumble............... 13
peppers
Chargrilled peppers................... 25
Gazpacho................................ 22
Indian vegetable curry............... 18
Oven-roasted vegetables 11
Panzanella 24
Ratatouille 21
Seven-vegetable tagine.............. 15
Stuffed peppers 33
Vegetable lasagna 20
Pesto, arugula & cilantro............. 62
pine nuts
Arugula & cilantro pesto........... 62
pineapple
Avocado & kiwi smoothie 83
pork
Cabbage & pork pot stickers 35
potatoes
Classic potato croquettes 1
French fries.............................. 2
Leek & potato soup................... 54
Oven-roasted vegetables 11
Patatas bravas 6
Potatoes dauphinoise 3
Potato gnocchi 7
Potato rösti 4
Potato smash 16
Roast potatoes......................... 5
prosciutto
Creamy mushroom sauce.......... 44
Pumpkin pie 79
purple sprouting broccoli
Stir-fried broccoli & kale.......... 38

R
Radicchio, chargrilled................. 64
Raisins, broccoli with 75
raspberries
Beet brownies 81

Beet, raspberry & mint juice 84
Ratatouille 21
Ravioli, butternut squash 30
rice
   Cabbage rolls............................ 34
   Wild mushroom risotto 46
ricotta
   Spinach & ricotta cannelloni 60
Risotto, wild mushroom.............. 46
Romano beans
   Minestrone soup 23
Rösti, potato 4
rutabaga
   Oven-roasted vegetables 11

s
Salad dressings...................57a, 57b
salad leaves 56a, 56b
salads
   Arugula & Parmesan salad 61
   Beet & cheese salad 14
   Fennel & Parmesan salad 42
salami
   Baked shallots........................... 53
Salsify & mackerel cakes............. 66
Samphire butter, beans with........ 72
sauces
   Arugula & cilantro pesto........... 62
   Creamy mushroom sauce.......... 44
   Tomato pasta sauce 19
Seven-vegetable tagine 15
Shallots, baked 53
smoked mackerel
   Salsify & mackerel cakes........... 66
smoked salmon
   Corn fritters 77
Smoothies 83
Snow peas, stir-fried.................... 73
soups
   Butternut squash soup 29
   Corn & chicken soup 76
   French onion soup 50
   Gazpacho 22
   Jerusalem artichoke soup 9
   Leek & potato soup.................. 54
   Minestrone soup 23
   Mushroom soup 47
   Pea & ham soup 69
   Sweet carrot soup 78
spinach
   Creamed spinach....................... 58
   Spinach & feta in phyllo 59
   Spinach & ricotta cannelloni......
  60

Spinach, orange & pear
   smoothie.................................. 83
   Vegetable lasagna 20
Sprouts with pancetta 37
squash
   Butternut squash ravioli 30
   Butternut squash soup 29
   Vegetable lasagna 20
strawberries
   Arugula & strawberry
   smoothie.................................. 83
sugar snap peas
   Pasta primavera 68
   Stir-fried snow peas.................. 73
Sweet carrot soup 80
sweet potatoes
   Indian vegetable curry.............. 18
   Oven-roasted vegetables 11
   Seven-vegetable tagine 15
   Sweet potato chips 12
   Sweet potato crumble............... 13
   Sweet potato mash 17
Swiss chard
   Indian vegetable curry.............. 18

t
Tagine, seven-vegetable 15
tagliatelle
   Pasta primavera 68
tahini
   Carrot hummus........................ 8
   Tahini cream........................... 57b
tarts
   Caramelized onion tart 52
   Onion flan............................... 51
   Pumpkin pie 79
Thai dressing 57a
Toasts, mushroom 48
tomatoes
   Braised Greek-style beans......... 74
   Cabbage rolls............................ 34
   Eggplant parmigiana 28
   Gazpacho 22
   Indian vegetable curry.............. 18
   Minestrone soup 23
   Panzanella 24
   Patatas bravas 6
   Quick gazpacho juice 84
   Ratatouille 21
   Seven-vegetable tagine 15
   Spinach & ricotta cannelloni...... 60
   Tomato pasta sauce 19
   Vegetable lasagna 20
Tzatziki 32

v
Vegetable lasagna 20
vinegar
   Artichokes with vinaigrette 40
   Balsamic dressing 57a
   Vinaigrette............................... 57b

w
walnuts
   Slow-cooked fennel 41
watermelon
   Beet, raspberry & mint
   juice 84
Wild mushroom risotto 46
wonton wrappers
   Butternut squash ravioli 30

y
Yakitori, mushroom...................... 49
yogurt
   Horseradish, chive & yogurt
   dressing 57b
   Tzatziki 32

z
zucchini
   Chocolate zucchini cake........... 82
   Indian vegetable curry.............. 18
   Ratatouille.............................. 21
   Seven-vegetable tagine 15
   Zucchini fritters....................... 26

ACKNOWLEDGMENTS

A million tablespoonfuls of gratitude to Catie Ziller — thanks for continuing to invite me back and allowing me to keep doing to do what I love. Oh, and for being a friend of genius, and for Paris and … no, I'd best not go on. All my respect and admiration goes to Alice Chadwick, who never ceases to inspire me with her wonderful final touches. I feel total admiration for my always reliable editor Kathy Steer — on whom I can always count — thanks for being the best backstop ever. I thank you Clive "Bozza" Hill for the photographs of all the dishes and your wonderful generosity. A lifetime of pork products and cheese for Kirsten Jenkins, my truly delightful friend and all grown-up "no more P Plates" home, etc. Thanks Kirst, for being all I believed you would be and then more. I shall never forget our amazing chorizo and red wine research trip to the Basque country.

Back in Australia, a massive thanks to the superbly talented Margarida Belleza for helping me taste and test every single recipe in this book, your input was invaluable, and thanks for sharing your pearls. And to conclude, to my family and dear friends, thanks for sending me emails and remembering I exist. To my divine friend Annie Mac for being the best source of friendship, inspiration and support I could ever wish for. I am forever indebted to you for your tireless efforts. Hopefully by the time you read this you will be sipping a cocktail by your gorgeous new pool. Kawika Boyce, bless you, for your massive heart and incredible devotion to me and my most cherished partner in crime, Pride Joy. I am so lucky to know someone else who will blend vegetables and barley for my pampered dog and not once complain or think me odd. And lastly, to my Pride Joy — ha ha, I finally got you eating vegetables and look how pretty and healthy you are now.